CUBA:

LIVING BETWEEN HURRICANES

CUBA:

LIVING BETWEEN HURRICANES

climate, commodities and sustainability

Jonathan Curry-Machado

amaurea

ISBN 978-1-914278-01-3

This book has been compiled as a companion volume to the documentary *Cuba: Living Between Hurricanes* (dir. Michael Chanan, 2019)
www.livingbetweenhurricanes.org

The film was funded by the UK Arts and Humanities Research Council (AHRC), and made under the aegis of the School of Advanced Study, University of London, for the Commodities of Empire British Academy Research Project (www.commoditiesofempire.org.uk), in collaboration with the *Fundación Antonio Núñez Jiménez de la Naturaleza y el Hombre* (Havana, Cuba) and the *Instituto Cubano del Arte e Industria Cinematográficos* (ICAIC).

Cover, book design & typesetting by Albarrojo
Published by Amaurea Press

Amaurea Press is an imprint of Amaurea Creative Productions Ltd.
London, United Kingdom
www.amaurea.co.uk

To the people of Caibarién
past, present and future

And all those who live between hurricanes

Contents

List of Illustrations

Preface

This book is the accompanying volume for the documentary *Cuba: Living Between Hurricanes*, directed by Michael Chanan, and written and produced by Jonathan Curry-Machado and Jean Stubbs. In 2019, with funding from the UK Arts and Humanities Research Council (AHRC), we travelled to Cuba in order to make a film that we originally thought would be about the interplay between hurricanes and commodities in the history of Cuba – in particular in the coastal town of Caibarién, on the north-central coast. What we found was a story that went beyond this, leading us to look at how the environment has been altered, and what changes are being made to enable sustainable futures. It became a story not so much about the impact of the ferocious storms that annually strike this part of the world, but rather about how communities live and survive between them.

During the filming, we carried out interviews with a number of people: some were experts in their respective fields – historians, meteorologists, geographers; others were local to Caibarién with first-hand experience of life there. This book, like the documentary upon which it is based, has been structured around their words.

Since the film was made, the world has been hit by the Covid-19 pandemic, which has had a devastating impact on Cuba. With its health system rising to the challenge but stretched and its economic lifeline of tourism brought to a halt, Cuba once again finds itself vulnerable and struggling to survive.

Introduction

Michael Chanan

Living Between Hurricanes is a film about the elements – hurricanes and rain, the sea and the earth – focused on the fishing port of Caibarién on the north coast of Cuba, a town which has seen better days. It's a film about the effects of climate across the centuries in a Caribbean island sucked into global markets for its commodity crops – tobacco, coffee, and above all sugar. How sugar changed the landscape, through deforestation, soil exhaustion and pollution. About the collapse of sugar and the encroachment of a new commodity market – tourism. About the growing threat from climate change, and the move towards reforestation, ecotourism and sustainable farming.

We found our title in a speech by Cuba's President, Miguel Díaz-Canel, to the meeting of Caribbean countries in Managua in 2019: "Living between hurricanes has conditioned our lives; it has modified our geographies and spurred our migrations. And it has also educated us in the need to further study the phenomena that afflict us and work to reverse their damage."

We chose Caibarién because this is where Hurricane Irma, one of the most powerful ever to sweep the Caribbean, made landfall in the early hours of 9th September 2017. Initial research threw up a variety of footage of the event on YouTube, and we knew there would be more. But this would only be our starting point. Our aim was the historical big picture, and the relation of hurricanes to other facets of climate and ecology in a vulnerable region whose economy was tied into global markets. Two of us already knew the locality, where forests and food self-sufficiency had given way to cattle ranching, tobacco cultivation, and increasingly during the nineteenth century, the sugarcane industry, with its railways and sugar mills. Caibarién, once a thriving entrepôt, offered a promising vantage point to test the historians' thesis about the advance of commodity frontiers – a process in which the twenty-first century has brought the encroachment of a new commodity in the form of mass tourism, which is equally at the mercy of global markets, and also has serious ecological effects.

Working with the *Fundación Antonio Núñez Jiménez* (FANJ, a Cuban NGO dedicated to environmentalism) gave us the opportunity to get away from the iconic imagery of a Caribbean paradise that communism has caught in an anachronistic time warp – the very imagery associated with the mass tourism whose growth since the 1990s has gone some way to replacing the foreign earnings lost when the sugar industry collapsed after the fall of the Soviet bloc. Our camera offered an unvarnished alternative perspective, as we filmed the streets of the town and surrounding countryside, visited one of the new hotels on the nearby keys, and then travelled to Artemisa province to visit a reforestation scheme, an eco-tourist centre and an example of sustainable farming. These scenes are complemented in the resulting film by archive footage from our other collaborator, the Cuban film institute (ICAIC).

For myself, the prospect of filming in Cuba in 2019 was rather different from when I first filmed there in the 1980s, shooting on 16 mm on television budgets. This time we were shooting on digital video funded by an academic grant on minimal funding. The difference is astounding. In 1987, our budget for a 40-minute film, if I recall correctly, was about £85 k, or around £245 k in today's money (according to the Bank of England inflation calculator). Our budget in 2019 was under £45 k.

Documentary power structures

The documentary filmmaker is situated within a power structure: in front of them is a certain reality to be put on the screen, which always remains fragmentary and elusive; looking over their shoulder is the institutional apparatus that provides the funding and the conditions for reaching the audience. The result is a double imbalance of power: on the one hand between filmmaker and subject; on the other, between filmmaker and funder. The relation between filmmaker and subject is a delicate and personal one, since each tends to become invested in the other; but the fact remains that the subject is handing their representation over to the filmmaker to make what they will of it, while the filmmaker's autonomy is tempered by the requirements of the funder. It makes a difference if the latter is a television executive or, as in this case, an academic funding body, which makes no editorial interventions. But that does not avoid the wider implications of the problem.

To interrogate this power grid, I turn to a conversation I had with Fredric Jameson a good many years ago, where he suggested considering documentary in terms of the different levels that shape the filmmaker's endeavour. The first level is the ostensive subject: a film about such-and-such, located in profilmic reality, and liable to invoke a number of clichés and commonplaces that normally obscure it. As Siegfried Kracauer once remarked: "In the illustrated magazines the public sees the world whose perception of it is hindered by the illustrated journals themselves."

There is then a second level, in which, as Jameson puts it, "what we're not seeing but what is present all the time... is the drama of the filmmaker" in the process of making the film. The documentarist is like "an actor who has a certain mission, so the... film can be seen as a kind of dramatic act in this larger, unfilmed story, which is this filmmaker doing something to the clichés or conventions". This larger story is unfilmed because it cannot be filmed because it happens off camera. Starting with Jean Rouch, documentarists have sought ways to make reflexive films that point to the fact of being filmed, edited, constructed, authored – but they can never tell all.

And then there's the third level, which is where the categories and conventions come from. Jameson is inclined to see this as a question of epistemology, of universals and categories and normative classifications, which derive from the increasingly complex organisation of knowledge; and this, he thinks, would be difficult for the documentarist to escape. Why? Because the categories are everywhere, and the portrayal of particulars cannot escape them. However, knowledge also serves as a means of power and control; in other words, it has an ideological dimension (or if you prefer, lends itself to ideological uses). What happens on the screen is that the particular is readily taken as a universal and can hardly avoid evoking connotations at once public and cultural. This also makes it ambiguous and open to interpretation, which occurs at all three levels, and by stages, from the act of filming to the moment of viewing.

I experienced all this afresh when shooting *Cuba: Living Between Hurricanes*. On the first, ostensive level, the basic problem is simply the limits of representation. As Bertolt Brecht put it (in a remark cited by Walter Benjamin), the simple reproduction of reality says very little about what it shows, and a photograph of, say, the Krupp works or AEG tells us almost nothing about these enterprises, because it cannot reveal the reification of human relations that is produced within them. So, for example, in the region around Caibarién, there are numerous symptoms of environmental degradation and damage, but they are not necessarily transparent to the camera. If you're not tutored in such things, how do you distinguish, just by looking at them, between buildings dilapidated by neglect and those suffering from hurricane damage? (And how to avoid aestheticising them?) Ecological damage can be even more problematic, like the beach that has been eroded and rebuilt by bringing in sand from somewhere else. These things need a narrative, and discursive knowledge, like a speaking voice to explain what we are seeing – and even if you can avoid an impersonal commentary, this inevitably throws the film back onto the established tropes and conventions of semantic domination. Avoiding or mitigating these stylistic automatisms is partly a matter of how you film and even more how you edit.

The second level – the story of the making of the film – threatened to derail us, because of the multilayered and parallel structures of authority, including the administrative bureaucracy, which is a characteristic of the Cuban political system. Perhaps we were being naive, despite our many collective years of experience of Cuba. We arrived in Caibarién and started filming; but on the third day, we were summoned to the local branch of the Interior Ministry. They took us for journalists and asked to see our visas, which had been issued on the basis that we are academics making an educational documentary. When we explained the difference, the affable officer who interviewed us agreed we could carry on.

The local government was a different matter. Although ICAIC had issued us with the required filming permission, which should have been communicated to the local authorities in Caibarién by way of the provincial authorities in Santa Clara, it hadn't reached them. We weren't sure why, but until this happened, the local authority in Caibarién would not give us their approval. It was difficult to gauge their thinking. For a couple of days we were followed around, so we restricted our filming to supposedly touristy scenes, delaying the interviews we wanted with local personalities; and then our fixer arranged for a couple of people to come to the hostel where we were staying instead of us going to them. In the end, despite the efforts of both our partner organisations, the required permission never came through, although this didn't stop us filming most of what we wanted.

People we interviewed were clearly sympathetic to our plight. Some speculated there might be someone in Santa Clara who had some reason to impede us. Others thought the local authority was afraid of things people might say on camera that could tarnish the town's image, or perhaps their own. Back in Havana another explanation emerged. There was indeed an issue between Caibarién and Santa Clara. The folk in Caibarién were resentful that Santa Clara put more resources into the nearby and older town of Remedios, where the buildings round the central square had been beautifully restored, but no equivalent work had been done in Caibarién. Whatever the explanation, it seemed to us that the weak bureaucratic need to assert control was driven by a certain paranoia, and this of course only produces more paranoia in those who brush up against it – including momentarily ourselves.

Local authority in Cuba is aligned and elided with the central authority of the (one-party) state, but there is evidently also a disconnect, which compounds the problem of the relation between the second and third levels mentioned earlier. If the interaction between the centralised state and what happens on the ground seems opaque, it also obscures the distinction between the drama of the filmmaker and the categories that constrain your efforts.

We had been caught up in an instance of this disconnect, which ironically also concerns the status of independent filmmaking in Cuba. Like everywhere else, digital videography has been flourishing in Cuba since the beginning of the millennium in the form of a lively and innovative independent film movement. Although ICAIC has provided a measure of support and cooperation, the independent filmmakers, many of them film-school graduates, occupied a kind of twilight zone in which they were neither legal (that is, recognised as self-employed, known as *cuentapropistas*) nor illegal. Back in 2013 the independents began to campaign, along with filmmakers belonging to the ICAIC, for a new law to recognise their work and provide appropriate support. A new law has finally been announced, and was published just after we arrived, and it appears to grant the main aims the filmmakers were campaigning for. But of course, it was not yet in operation, and at times we felt that we too occupied a parallel zone of ill-defined status.

The film

The film combines a series of elements, including the benefit of access to the archive at the Cuban Cinemateca, especially the newsreels that ICAIC released every week from 1960 to 1990, which provide glimpses of hurricanes and their aftermath, as well as various aspects of agro-industry. My particular thanks to Dolores Calviño for the preselection of the footage. The independent filmmaker Giselle García Castro kindly gave us drone shots of Caibarién filmed for her documentary *Lista Quinta*.

Our interlocutors fall into two main groups. First, the historians and others who gathered for a symposium hosted by FANJ in Havana. Second, the people we met in Caibarién, who were well aware of being caught between the past, which has bequeathed problems like soil exhaustion and contamination, and a future threatened by rising temperatures and sea levels combined with ever more intense hurricanes. Our guide in Caibarién was a local ecological activist, Pedro González. Reinaldo Funes from the FANJ took us to the eco-tourist installation at Las Terrazas, near Havana, and not far away, Finca Marta, a model of sustainable farming run by his brother Fernando Funes. My special thanks to all three of them.

The resulting film is intended to support the FANJ's work within Cuba and connect it to an international audience geared up to thinking globally and acting locally. Disseminated through open access (www.livingbetweenhurricanes.org) it was made with funding from the UK's Arts and Humanities Research Council (AHRC), under aegis of the Commodities of Empire British Academy Research Project at the University of London's School of Advanced Studies, with project partners in the UK, USA, Puerto Rico, Spain and the Netherlands – one of many networks now influencing public thinking and policy makers at both local and international level.

Participants

This book has been largely put together from transcripts of the interviews given for the *Cuba: Living Between Hurricanes* documentary. They have been linked in such a way as to tell the story – one that is close to that of the documentary itself, although with added details. The following are the interviewees, who are identified throughout the text with their initials.

Armando Caymares (AC)
A widely-respected Cuban meteorologist, and leading specialist at the Institue of Meteorology in Havana, working in the National Forecast Centre.

Armando Fernández Soriano (AF)
A geo-historian based at the *Fundación Antonio Núñez Jiménez* in Havana, where he works within the Geohistorical Research Programme. He is the co-editor of the book *An Island in the Stream: Ecocritical and Literary Responses to Cuban Environmental Culture.*

Abel Arnaldo González López (AAG)
Born and brought up in Caibarién, but now living in Havana. Having trained as a pychologist he now works as a tourist guide, travelling to every part of Cuba.

Angel Luis Díaz Cabezas (ALD)
A self-taught Caibarién-based artist, known for his stone sculptures. A mason by trade, he has been involved in the restoration and repair of some of Caibarién's historic buildings – including that of the Caibarién branch of the Union of Writers and Artists (UNEAC), of which he is an office bearer.

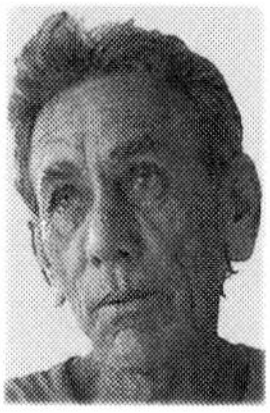

Alejandro Morffi González (AM)
A native of Caibarién, who has lived his whole life there. He is a pioneering explorer of the local area, and concerned observer of the local environment; as well as a leading member of the Caibarien Speleological Society, with which he has made numerous discoveries of pre-columbian remains.

Angel Omar Vara San Juan (AOV)
Director of the Museum of Traditions in Caibarién, and a native of the city. He is a specialist on the socio-cultural life of the town, in particular the *parrandas* – the popular festivals for which Caibarién, Remedios and other communities in the region are famed.

Ana Vera Estrada (AVE)
A cultural and oral history specialist, based at the Juan Marinello Institute for Cultural Research in Havana. She has carried out extensive research into the experiences of former sugar communities around Cuba.

Fernando Funes Monzote (FF)
A Cuban agro-ecologist. Having studied production ecology and resource conservation in Spain and the Netherlands, he founded the Finca Marta farm, west of Havana – named after his mother, Marta Monzote, herself a pioneer in sustainable agriculture.

Hernán Venegas (HV)
A Cuban historian, now based in Mexico. He is a specialist in regional histories, and has extensively researched the past of central Cuba.

Luis Enrique Ramos Guadalupe (LER)
A Cuban meteorological historian. Founding member of the Cuban Meteorological Society, and member of the International Commission on Meteorological History. Author of *Father Benito Viñes: The 19th-Century Life & Contributions of a Cuban Hurricane Observer & Scientist.*

Liliana Núñez Velis (LN)
A Cuban environmental historian, and President of the Fundación Antonio Núñez Jiménez.

Manuel Iturralde-Vinent (MI)
A Cuban geologist and palaeontolgist, formerly deputy director of the Cuban National Natural History Museum in Havana. He has carried out many studies of Cuban and Caribbean geology, palaentology and caves.

Martín Núñez Rodríguez (MN)
A native of Caibarién, where he works as a meteorological observer at the town's weather station, and teaches courses locally on geography.

Mireya Pérez (MP)
A native of Caibarién. Formerly an engineer at the Marcelo Salado sugar factory, she continued working there as a specialist after it was converted into a Sugar Museum. She now gives guided tours of the installations to visitors.

Natalia Quintana Díaz (NQ)
A native of Caibarién, who has lived her whole life there. She is a cultural specialist and community organiser, working closely with the small rural community of Dolores.

Oscar Zanetti Lecuona (OZ)
A renowned Cuban historian, formerly Director of the Institute of History in Havana. He has specialised in particular in the history of the Cuban sugar industry. He has widely published, both nationally and internationally, and his books include *Sugar and Railroads.*

***Pedro Manuel González Reinoso* (PG)**
A native of Caibarién, where he continues to live. An environmental activist and independent journalist, reporting on the social and ecological problems faced by his community. Member of the *Guardabosques* environmental action organisation.

***Reinaldo Funes Monzote* (RF)**
Director of the Geohistorial Research Programme at the *Fundación Antonio Núñez Jiménez*, and Professor of History at the University of Havana. His publications include *From Rainforest to Cane Field: An Environmental History since 1492.*

***Raúl Rodríguez Cabrera* (RR)**
A native of Caibarién, where he works as a specialist in socio-cultural studies. He is the Director of Artistic Projects in the town, as well as the representative and coordinator of the *Grupo de Rumba* 'Obbá Ewé'.

***Sherry Johnson* (SJ)**
Professor of History at Florida International University. Her research focuses in particular on 18th-century Cuba, with a special interest in the impact of climatic events. Her books include *Climate and Catastrophe in Cuba and the Atlantic World in the Age of Revolution.*

CUBA:

LIVING BETWEEN HURRICANES

Map of Cuba, showing Caibarién
Source: University of Texas Libraries

Present-day Caibarién seen from the air
Aerial photograph by Ariel Suárez, courtesy of Giselle García Castro

Living between hurricanes has conditioned our lives;
it has modified our geographies and spurred our migrations.
And it has also educated us in the need to further study the phenomena
that afflict us and work to reverse their damage.

Cuban President Miguel Díaz-Canel

1 Irma and Caibarién

The psychological state of people changes when a hurricane approaches and the weather deteriorates. When the centre of the hurricane arrives, the wind gust is intense, and everything is a dark grey. People start to get nervous. And there is also a strange smell. It is something we always remember from childhood. When there is a very intense wind, a hurricane capable of ripping off branches, leaves from the trees, and it seems even the sap, all this destroyed organic material becomes impregnated in the rain like an aerosol, and so there is a smell like fresh green leaves. Like the smell of a grove. Also, on the coast, the wind brings salt from the sea, which can penetrate inland. This is typical of hurricanes. This is the strange smell that many people speak of when a hurricane passes.

Armando Caymares

In September 2017, one of the most powerful hurricanes ever to sweep the Caribbean made landfall in north-central Cuba. Images of the devastation of the coastal town of Caribarién were broadcast around the world, bringing back to international prominence a port that had once thrived with the export of sugar and tobacco, and as a centre for fishing, but which has long since fallen into decline.

As the *Associated Press* reported on 10th September 2017:

Hurricane Irma ripped roofs off houses, collapsed buildings and flooded hundreds of miles of coastline as it raked Cuba after cutting a trail of destruction across the Caribbean. As Irma left Cuba and directed its 130 mph winds towards Florida, authorities on the island were warning of staggering damage to keys along the northern coast studded with all-inclusive resorts and cities, as well as farmland in central Cuba. There were no immediate reports of deaths in Cuba – a country that prides itself on its disaster preparedness – but authorities were trying to restore power, clear roads and warning that people should stay off the streets of Havana because flooding could continue. Government news website *Cubadebate* said evacuations across the island totalled over one-million people. Emergency workers in inflatable boats navigated flooded streets along Havana's coastline, where thousands of people left their homes for safer ground. Seawater penetrated as much as 1,600 feet inland. Trees toppled, roofs were torn off, cement water tanks fell from roofs to the ground and electrical lines are down. As Irma rolled in, Cuban soldiers went through coastal towns to force residents to evacuate, taking people to shelters at government buildings and schools – even caves. In Caibarién, a small coastal city about 200 miles east

Satellite image of Hurricane Irma (9th September 2017)
Source: US National Oceanic and Atmospheric Administration

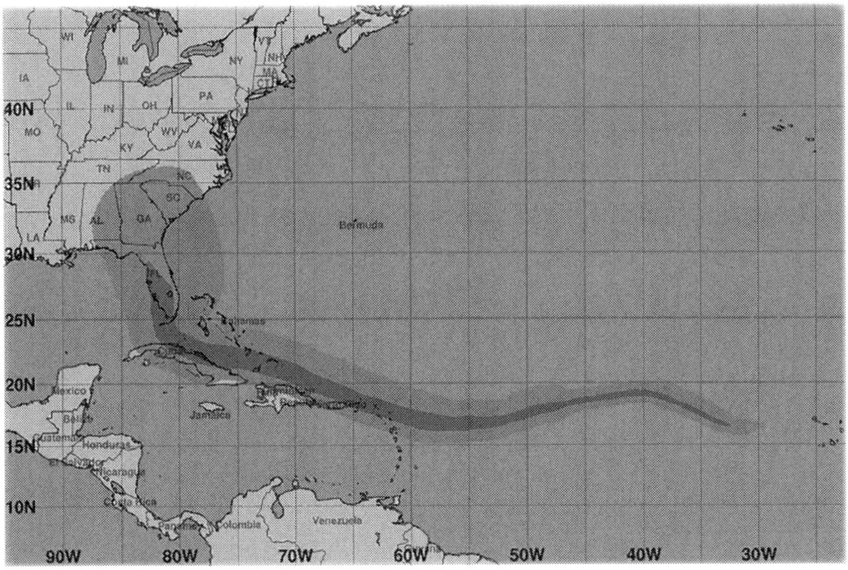

Trajectory of Hurricane Irma (August – September 2017)

Source: US National Weather Service – National Hurricane Center

of Havana, winds downed power lines and neighbourhoods were under water. Many residents stayed put, hoping to ride out the storm.

Cuba had been forewarned. Irma had already wreaked a path of destruction across the Caribbean. The National Hurricane Center in Miami had begun monitoring the tropical depression from which it grew on 26th August, over western Africa. During the next few days this coalesced, in the vicinity of the Cape Verde Islands. By 31st August, it had become a Category 3 hurricane. In Cuba a wary eye was kept on the storm as it progressed; and as it drew nearer, the population were kept fully informed.

AC:
When a tropical cyclone is to the east of the curve of the Lesser Antilles, tropical cyclone warnings are given at six in the evening every twenty-four hours. When the hurricane passes fifty-five degrees west, then the frequency of the warnings is every twelve hours: at six in the morning and six in the evening. When the hurricane is seventy-two hours away, the tropical cyclone warning is given every six hours. And then when the danger is imminent, when it is very close to the territory, the warning is given every three hours.

As it approached the northern Leeward Islands on 5th September, Irma continued to intensify, becoming the first Category 5 storm on record to hit there. Although surpassed two years later by Hurricane Dorian, at the time it was believed to be the strongest ever in the open Atlantic region. It caused catastrophic damage over the islands of Barbuda, Saint Berthelemy, Saint Martin, Anguilla and the Virgin Islands. A state of emergency was declared in Puerto Rico, and although it actually passed to the north of the island, considerable damage was caused. By 7th September, it was grazing the Dominican Republic and Haiti, both of which sustained heavy winds and rains. It became very clear that Cuba was going to be next.

AC:
On 5th September, internally it was thought by national defence and those organisations involved in the early warning system, that there was a high probability that Irma would hit the north coast of Cuba. I told a friend who works in Radio Caibarién, on the 5th or 6th September I think, that 'you are going to have problems, it's possible you will have it from the 9th. The direct impact is going to pass very close to Caibarién'. Which it in fact did. It was going to penetrate Cuban national territory and, approximately four days beforehand, the authorities were notified of the potential danger.

As official warnings mounted of the imminent arrival of Irma, the inhabitants of Caibarién began to prepare themselves to bear the brunt of the storm.

PG:
We had already spent twenty-four hours without electricity. They switched the current off the previous day, as we prepared for the hurricane to hit. So, I went out to buy water and food, knowing what was coming.

AC:
When the winds start to have speeds averaging 80 kph, the electric current is switched off, and anyone who doesn't have a battery can't find out what is happening. In order to get through a hurricane, you need to have light food, so as to be seven days without electricity, without any service of any kind.

AM:
From the first warning, the preparations were immense. Neighbours were asking me about the possible effects, so I warned them.

Cuba's Institute of Meteorology kept the storm under full surveillance throughout, as they do for all such weather-related events, and the Cuban public were kept fully informed of the hurricane's progress.

AC:
The hurricane connected with Cuba at three points. It penetrated at 9pm in the vicinity of Cayo Romano, exiting below Cayo Coco. During the early hours, it crossed what is known as Buenavista Bay, which is an open bay to the north, between Caibarién and Cayo Santa María. Then it crossed the north of Villa Clara, passing over a coastal zone of the Encrucijada municipality. From there it started moving west or west-northwest, and left the north-eastern edge of Villa Clara, very close to Matanzas province, in the area of Carahatas – a locality to the west of Sagua la Grande. It then started moving west-northwest, with some north-westerly tendencies, with the area of hurricane-force winds distancing from Cuba during the 10th.

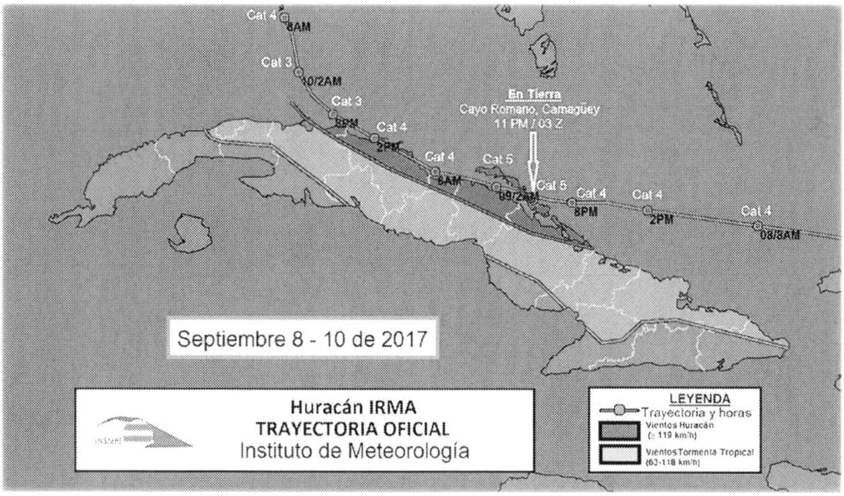

Path of Irma as it hit Cuba (September 2017)
Source: Instituto de Meteorología, Cuba

It was very clear that Irma was a hurricane of historic proportions.

LER:
The fundamental difference between Irma and the other hurricanes that have passed over these zones in the last century lies in its intensity. Irma was a hurricane that for a time reached Category 5 on the Saffir-Simpson scale, which is the maximum.

This was only the second hurricane ever confirmed to have made landfall in Cuba as a Category 5 storm, with wind speeds in excess of 156 mph (the other being the 1924 'Cuba' hurricane). With wind intensity reaching 180 mph, Irma became – along with 1998's Hurricane Mitch and 2005's Hurricane Rita – the sixth-strongest Atlantic hurricane on record.

Strongest recorded Atlantic hurricanes

	SUSTAINED WIND SPEEDS (mph)	PRESSURE (hPa)
Allen, 1980	190	899
Wilma, 2005	185	882
Gilbert, 1988	185	888
'Labor Day', 1935	185	892
Dorian, 2019	185	910
Rita, 2005	180	895
Mitch, 1998	180	905
Irma, 2017	**180**	**914**
Camille, 1969	175	900
Katrina, 2005	175	902
Dean, 2007	175	905
Maria, 2017	175	908
Janet, 1955	175	914
Santa Cruz del Sur, 1932	175	915
Andrew, 1992	175	922
David, 1979	175	924
Anita, 1977	175	926
Felix, 2007	175	929

AC:
Irma was a large hurricane, and the tropical storm-strength winds covered an area of 315 km from the centre. That is, the whole of Cuba would have tropical storm-strength winds. Also, the hurricane moved at around 20 km per hour, which brought hurricane-force winds to the north coast and the municipalities of Villa Clara for a period in excess of ten to twelve hours. There was also a prolonged period of intense rains, above all on the right-hand side of the trajectory, in some places with between 250 and 500 mm falling. The rain was particularly copious in mountainous zones, and also in parts of the north coast, such as Caibarién and the Remedios area, where the rain was extremely heavy.

Hurricanes are a dynamic phenomenon. When they touch land, friction causes the winds to start depleting. The structure of the hurricane becomes eroded, and so the hurricane-force winds begin to contract. And that is one characteristic of Hurricane Irma. It became asymmetric as it penetrated into the north of Camagüey and Ciego de Ávila. The area of hurricane-force winds (that is those over 74 mph) began to reduce, and the hurricane-force area along the north coast of Cuba began to narrow.

It should be remembered that a hurricane is not a single point. A hurricane is a system. And what is followed is the centre of the hurricane. Logically around the centre, to a radius of approximately 100 or 150 km, the most intense winds are concentrated. This is called the 'destructive ring'. The most intense winds and rain are in what is known as the inner nucleus, or eye, of the hurricane. Outside the hurricane there are the external spiral bands, which bring heavy rain and electric storms. There might also be associated tornados. And the weather gradually deteriorates. But when the eye of the hurricane arrives, the weather deteriorates very rapidly, in a question of minutes. The wind gusts bring sudden increases in wind velocity.

There might also be tornados and severe storms within the eye of the hurricane. There can be electric storms, produced within the storm clouds, above all lightning within the hurricane's eye; and at night continuous electric activity can be seen, above all in hurricanes that are in the process of intensifying.

Devastating though the winds and rain undoubtedly were, what made the experience of Irma all the more impactful was how slowly it moved.

AC:
This hurricane had two characteristics. It was an intense hurricane, maintaining that intensity for a long period of time. And also, it was a very large hurricane. It touched the zone of Cayo Romano as a Category 5. While moving along the northern zone of Caibarién, it was between Category 4 and 3 on the Saffir-Simpson scale. And then when it was in the north-east of Villa Clara it was a Category 3. That is, it was weakening. Of course, it was a large hurricane, and large hurricanes don't weaken easily. The north of Villa Clara suffered hurricane-strength winds for many hours, during practically the whole of the 9th September.

What happened is that by the end of the 9th September, on changing its direction the hurricane reduced greatly its speed of movement. So the whole of that northern part of central Cuba, through the 9th and 10th, was directly affected by this powerful hurricane.

The strongest winds are always on the right-hand side of the centre. These were felt in Cayo Coco, in Cayo Romano, in the area of Punta Alegre. But according to the satellite images, the strongest wind gusts were always over the sea, in the Old Bahama Channel and the Florida Straits. That was fortunate. Nevertheless, the meteorological stations recorded a maximum gust of 256 kph in a locality in the north of Ciego de Avila, and the winds in the Caibarién area were around 180, 190 kph, with gusts in Caibarién of 215 kph.

Street scene, Caibarién in the aftermath of Irma (September 2017)

Image taken from film *Cuba: Living Between Hurricanes*

Such technical details do little to describe the actual impact that the storm had for those living through it in Caibarién.

RR:
It was an unforgettable experience. It was my wife's birthday, and it was terrible. What with the wind, and all that was happening. Irma lasted almost twenty-four hours, with sustained winds.

ALD:
My experience with the hurricane? Well, it was terrible. The winds were very strong. Even though we protected the building, there was damage. A tank was blown loose on the roof, and its water damaged the upper floors. Some tiles fell. The building was completely soaked, because the water came with a lot of wind. There were leaks because of the strong wind. Some of the glass was broken. In my house, the roof almost completely went. It was a strong hurricane.

MN:
It was my responsibility to go to the meteorological station, because I am a meteorological observer. But because I have an elderly mother, they let me stay with her. I experienced the effects of the hurricane in my house. I could see how it was lifting the tiles from the roofs opposite. I heard the loud crash caused by the falling of the cinema that used to be here. Its roof collapsed. I took my mother to the house next door, which was more strongly built. My house lost a few tiles, but it held up.

In a report in *Cubadebate*, on 10th September, a Caibarién resident, Marta Marrero, commented:

> As the wind increased in intensity, we saw how the roof gave signs that it would be ripped off at any moment. There was an instant in which we were afraid for our lives, with the impossibility of going out into the street to take shelter in another house. My son decided to open a hole of about 50 cm in the wall, and through there we were able to get into the neighbouring house.

Such experiences of surviving the hurricane were commonplace, with so much of the town suffering damage.

Home destroyed by Irma, Caibarién (September 2017)
Photo: Pedro Manuel González Reinoso

PG:
I remember being in my house with my parents, alone with them. I live in a building amongst those that were built in the seventies, on the ground floor. They have a very resistant structure, because they were made with genuine cement. What suffered most in my building were the windows, which were rather old. Some of them didn't withstand the strength of the winds. Luckily, I have the ground floor, where although the windows are as old as those above, the higher floors suffer more because they are less surrounded by buildings that protect them. I didn't suffer greatly. Some meshes were pulled off of a window, which I myself had to hold onto during the hurricane. At seven in the morning there was a thunderous wind. I thought I would be blown away with all of it. I had put some black plastic bags over the windows, mainly because of the rain, because with the wind the slats were letting a stream of water into the house. There was a moment in which I believed the windows were going to fly off, and I had to hang onto them to stop it. A frame became unstuck from one window. But that is nothing compared to what the rest of the people in the municipality suffered.

AM:
My house suffered immense damage, and like mine there are two-thousand houses in Caibarién that suffered severely. We have never been through such a difficult experience. Here we had never been so severely affected, so disastrously.

ALD:
I lived through Hurricane Kate [1985], and this was much stronger than Kate. It lasted a lot longer. I thought it was never going to end. It arrived during the night, and at six in the morning it was still here. I felt afraid, because I was with my wife and daughter. There were moments when if you touched the walls, it felt as though they were moving, and that at any moment the roof would go. Because they were very strong winds. Too strong.

Further along the coast, as Irma continued her progression westwards, the impact of the storm continued to be felt – and as with most hurricanes, everyone subsequently had their individual story to tell.

Building damage from Irma, Caibarién (September 2017)
Photo: Pedro Manuel González Reinoso

AF:
It's important to consider at what time the event occurs. I believe nocturnal hurricanes leave a deeper impression. I say this because I spent Irma in Varadero, where it passed during the night. It stayed twelve hours there without moving, almost on the tip of the peninsular, 36 km away. And it was night-time. It was impressive to hear. The noise of the water. The sea. It seemed to roar. They even started to evacuate people. I hid on the second floor, with my dog. I switched off the lights of the lantern, and I stayed hiding there, because I wasn't going to leave the dog alone in the house.

AC:
As the wind speed increases, there is a notable increase in the dynamic push of the wind against flat structures, and so very intense hurricane winds are very dangerous. The hurricane-speed winds produce the fall of trees, they break branches from trees, cause electric and telephone pylons to collapse. They remove the coverings from structurally weak houses.

Not only did falling trees cause further damage to structures, as well as increase the risk to human life, but the obstruction they caused in the streets, parks and other public spaces impeded the natural drainage of the water, thereby increasing the incidence of flooding. It was of course those who were closest to the coast that felt the most powerful effects, as the hurricane-force winds raised the sea, producing storm surges often more damaging than the winds themselves.

LER:
Irma generated a strong chain of coastal floods along the length of its passage through the keys, or islands, in the north-central region of Cuba.

AC:
What is bad about hurricanes is the vulnerability of the buildings, since some are weak. In coastal settlements, like the city of Caibarién, which is practically just a few metres above sea level, we know that in some sectors the sea penetrated some five-hundred metres inland, almost half-a-kilometre.

Thankfully, following the flooding caused by the previous hurricane that caused devastating damage in Caibarién (Hurricane Kate, in 1985), a sea wall had been built to protect the town from incursions by the sea. As a result of this, the impact of Irma was not as grave as it could have been.

AM:
The sea level rose to a height of approximately one metre. Thanks to the sea wall, despite people criticising it, the influx from the waves was held back quite a bit.

PG:
In the low zones near the sea wall, I have some friends who lost everything. The sea rose in those places. It was very concentrated, it seems, because of the winds. And then the water stayed there. But the sea didn't sweep the town, like the last time.

But while a sea wall may provide some measure of protection, with storm surges of the magnitude seen during Irma, little could be done to prevent severe flooding. In the capital itself, Havana, although escaping the direct hit from Irma that Caibarién suffered, the impact of the raised sea level was felt, and caused substantial damage.

AC:
In Havana, many people living between 5th Street and Malecón didn't remove their cars. They left them there, and they lost them. Many people didn't evacuate, and many people said, 'they didn't tell me it was going to be like this.' Really? Because you don't see the television, the radio, you don't have a phone? Because the situation that the low parts of Vedado went through was terrible. There are those who lost everything: mattresses, pans, radio, television, they lost everything. But ever since it touched land at Cayo Coco, we knew that there were going to be waves estimated at between five and seven metres along the Havana waterfront. And the largest wave was 9.5 metres, to the north of Havana. Such waves on the Malecón are highly destructive.

For the inhabitants of Caibarién, Irma brought back uncomfortable memories of the last time the town suffered such a direct hit.

MN:
Hurricane Irma was the strongest that has affected this central-north region of Cuba. The last was in 1985, which was Hurricane Kate, but that was a Category 2. Irma hit us here as a Category 4 on the Saffir-Simpson scale, and the peculiarity that we lived was that as its trajectory followed the north coast, its speed of displacement diminished, and so strong winds were maintained with that intensity for many hours.

In our locality, they were in excess of 200 kph. As a result, the residential, industrial and social buildings of the city were very damaged, made worse by the associated rain and the slight penetration of the sea along the whole coastline.

Another Caibarién resident, Raúl Negrín, commented to the *Cubadebate* journalist who reported from the town on 10th September:

> Many people have compared it with Hurricane Kate, because these were the two strongest natural phenomena that we have experienced here. But that of the last few hours is unequalled. These several hours of strong winds, the constant rain and the assault of the sea are things that in my 65 years of life I have never seen with such intensity. The wind blew from many directions, and this all resulted in so much destruction.

Having made it through the stormy night, people emerged the next morning to observe the impact that Irma had left in its wake.

MN:
Afterwards, the following day, I went out. I took some photographs of the town, showing the impact of this intense hurricane, and I really saw the state of desolation. That's a good description, because of the great number of houses without roofs because of the hurricane, the electric lines on the ground. Some parts were still flooded, because the sea and the rain had not yet entirely receded. We were left without electric power, and so the most important places, like the hospitals, aqueduct and so on, were working with generators, but the rest of the population was without electricity.

PG:
The impact of the wind was notable, very devastating. When I went out to look around the town, under the rain, only a few hours after the hurricane had left heading towards Varadero and Cárdenas, there was still a wind speed of 120 kph. I almost couldn't go out into the street to film and see all that had happened. I felt devastated because I went past the homes of people that I knew, who were sitting in their doorways without roofs, everything soaked, and they didn't know what was going to happen.

RR:
Irma left its mark on Caibarién, with the destruction of many of our cultural buildings. And also personally. My house suffered a great deal. We've now been able to more or less rebuild it. When we went out into the streets of Caibarién the following day, the America Cinema [one of three that Caibarién once had, now all closed] had fallen down. The buildings near the port, which had been badly affected by the flooding, had fallen. That gives you a sense of how strong the winds were.

The abandoned Caibarién Cinema (2019)
Photo: Gonzalo Vidal

Warehouse damaged by Hurricane Irma, Caibarién (September 2017)
Photo: Pedro Manuel González Reinoso

AOV:
Nature, the trees, all that was beautiful, that were points of reference for us, they came down, and it was lamentable. I'm quite sensitive to these things. Going around and seeing those trees destroyed, it hit me hard.

PG:
The electrical infrastructure was destroyed, completely on the ground. The images were Dantesque. There was no energy to pump the water. So, there was no water in the pipes. But many people succeeded in storing water in their houses, to cover essentials: in the kitchen, the bathroom, and so on.

But there was an awareness that the impact, though considerable, was not as severe as it could very easily have been. With its history of withstanding hurricanes, and a government committed to proactive emergency response and disaster mitigation, although there was no way to avoid the material costs, the human toll was minimised. Across Cuba, 10 deaths were attributed to the hurricane, mainly in Havana – which was a far lower fatality rate than that experienced elsewhere, such as in the US with its 92 lives lost. Caibarién itself suffered no such loss. A local resident, Rosa González, when interviewed for *Cubadebate* on 10th September, noted that:

> Although we had considerable damage, it would have all been worse if we had a disorganised system. I was one of those evacuated, ahead of the risk, to the house of my relations; and although I lost a lot of tiles and even at one moment thought that nothing would survive, I've now come home, and I find almost everything there. In part that is due to the protective measures learned during so many years.

However, for a country already coping with severe material shortages, recovery from the storm was likely to take time.

Tree felled by Irma, Caibarién (September 2017)
Photo: Pedro Manuel González Reinoso

PG:
Caibarién suffered, as did almost the whole of the north-east of Cuba, the centre and parts of the west. It desolated many coastal populations, and produced one of the great disasters of last year. It started on 7th September 2017, and in 2018 we still hadn't recovered from that devastation. It came on top of previous difficulties. 2018 dawned with a desolate view. Three, four months had gone by since the hit. Infrastructure suffered, the population suffered under those magnificent winds. From a geographic point of view, it was a perfect phenomenon.

MN:
Immediately after the hurricane passed, you know that in our country there exists what is known as the 'Civil Defence', and a period of recovery was begun. Areas were prioritised that were important for satisfying the most pressing necessities of the population in that moment. The bakeries continued functioning, and the hospital, with electric generators.

PG:
We recovered very quickly in some things, but not in terms of electricity. The town's power lines took a bit longer to repair.

Damaged buildings, Caibarién (2019) (this page and opposite)
Photos: Gonzalo Vidal

MN:
The recovery of the electric system took several days. Here the electric lines are situated above ground, and were directly affected by the winds, so the network took quite a few days to be fixed, due to the large amount of work that needed to be done. Not only in this region. You have to remember that the hurricane affected almost the whole of the north-centre of the island, and so a lot of effort was needed for the recovery. Even though brigades came from other provinces that had been less affected, it still took several days to recover the electric power.

ALD:
After the hurricane, those of us who worked at the UNEAC building tried to solve our own problems, because we saw that the government was concentrating on dealing with other things. There were many people who had suffered a lot of damage. The town was completely damaged. There were things that we couldn't sort out, because that depends on having materials, and the government had to provide those. But we did what we could. We put the glass that had survived back into the windows, fixed doors that had become loose, and so on.

UNEAC building, Caibarién (2019)
Photo: Gonzalo Vidal

PG:
Some people recovered better than others, because of their possibilities for receiving help, in particular from their families outside Cuba. Everyone showed a lot of solidarity, sending money, sending medicine. Food as well, but anyway this was a zone that was given a high priority by the government for food distribution. That had to be done on a daily basis, because we had no means of refrigeration. What was bought had to be eaten on the same day. There was no way to store it. And so there was a continuous flow of lorries bringing stuff.

AM:
Much of the recovery was very quick. For example, the collection of rubbish, of debris, none of that took long. The electricity took longer. It was restored in sixteen days. It was badly damaged, but in sixteen days it recovered. But housing and state buildings, places of work, those still show problems. Lack of resources. A lack of control in the reception and dispatch of materials. But things have advanced. There are still difficulties. It was a tough blow.

Also, this hurricane was peculiar in that it affected practically the whole of the north coast of the island, from the centre to the west, because it was a big hurricane. Nearly the whole of the central-north coast of Cuba was affected, and that has made recovery harder. But well, we have recovered, although there are still difficulties. There are things that because of poor administration, poor control, haven't been able to be done. And others because of the reality of the lack of materials, of resources.

PG:
Some people in these outlying areas never succeeded in recovering. That is, today they are still trying to repair what was broken. But it came on top of the deterioration caused by years of neglect. I can say that there has been an increasing loss, unfortunately, of the heritage and architecture of the city.

AZUCARES

Ruined buildings in Caibarién (2019) (this page and opposite)
Photos: Gonzalo Vidal

2 A History of Hurricanes

Hurricanes have passed into Cuban culture, in numerous works of music, visual arts, theatre and above all literature. There is a strong presence of the hurricane as an object of interest for all those who have been writing in the last five centuries about Cuba and its culture.

Luis Enrique Ramos Guadalupe

The Caribbean Basin has always been prone to hurricanes, and these extreme weather events have played an important role throughout Cuban history.

LER:
Hurricanes have formed a part of Cuban history ever since the Cuban archipelago was populated by the original peoples who occupied this geographic space. The memory that remains of that first era is in the chronicles of the first European sailors who arrived in Cuba, and conquered the Caribbean area. There are references to sculptures made by the aborigines that reflect through their deities and mythological figures that aboriginal culture relating to hurricanes, and to natural phenomena in general.

In fact, the word we still use to describe these massive storms comes from the Tainos, who inhabited Cuba before the arrival of the Spanish.

A hurricane in the Caribbean, line engraving (late-16th century)
Source: Sarin Images/Granger

They had a god named Huracán, portrayed as having two arms in counter-clockwise rotation, just like the spiral cyclonic pattern we have since become very familiar with. Stuart Schwartz, in his history of hurricanes in the Caribbean, *Sea of Storms*, notes the familiarity the original peoples of the islands had with these events: "Europeans relied on Indians to tell them when hurricanes were coming".

> *LER:*
> For the Spanish who conquered Cuba, hurricanes were important as they put in danger their shipping, which was the connection between Europe and the Americas.

While such dangers were generally seen as something of a curse, that restricted sea travel during several months of the year out of fear of shipwreck, on occasions the storms proved to be a blessing. They could provide unexpected protection from would-be marauders, as in 1640, when the Dutch attempted to take Havana, but their fleet was destroyed by a hurricane.

> *HV:*
> From the seventeenth century in particular, information is found in the chronicles of the Indies about facing up to hurricanes, storms, etcetera.

Caibarién is fortunate that a local doctor, José A. Martínez-Fortún, took it upon himself, in the first half of the twentieth century, to write a multi-volume chronicle of life and events in the Remedios district, where Caibarién is situated. This includes a record of weather conditions – and particularly when something noteworthy occurred. The chronicle shows that, in 1712, a rainstorm caused damage in the fields, and again two years later. In 1734, storms affected the plantations of the vicinity, and again in 1751 and 1756. And so on, throughout the eighteenth century: notable storms again in 1775, 76, 78, 80 and 84; while those of 1794 were linked to a prevalence that year of yellow fever.

But alternating with these storms, the ever-present effect of droughts can also be seen.

> *SJ:*
> Scientists have long suspected that there is a relationship between hurricanes, El Niño and drought. In the Caribbean during the El Niño phase, usually the phenomenon is characterised by extensive drought. There is also a definite correlation between the El Niño and the lack of intensity or the diminution in intensity in the Caribbean, of hurricanes. The number of days and the intensity. Additionally, with La Niña, there seems to be a slight increase in the frequency of hurricanes and the intensity.

El Niño and La Niña are climate patterns caused, respectively, by warmer or colder ocean temperatures in the Pacific; but their effects are felt globally, and they have a significant impact on weather patterns in the Caribbean. These conflicting tendencies alternate with one another, in an irregular cycle known as El Niño Southern Oscillation (ENSO).

SJ:
We can look historically at how many hurricanes have hit Cuba, and then go to the historical documentation and try to see if we can find consequences; or if we can find evidence of both El Niño and La Niña in droughts and in increased hurricanes. To that end, my research has worked on demonstrating the effect of this fifty-year period of the late-eighteenth century, in which there were El Niño and La Niña events not only sequentially, but the changeover happened very, very quickly. Which is critical, because if you have an ecosystem stressed, and an El Niño condition, with drought, and then all of a sudden you go quickly into a La Niña circumstance in which you have torrential rainfall on a system that's already in crisis, it magnifies the effect on the people. The effect is massive flooding, the washing out of crops, animals drown, people drown, houses washed away. And ultimately people have to decide whether they're going to stay and try to rebuild, or will migrate.

In 1735, an intense drought in the first months of the year badly affected the cattle herds of the area; while in 1756, another long drought had a serious impact on the local economy; and again in 1783.

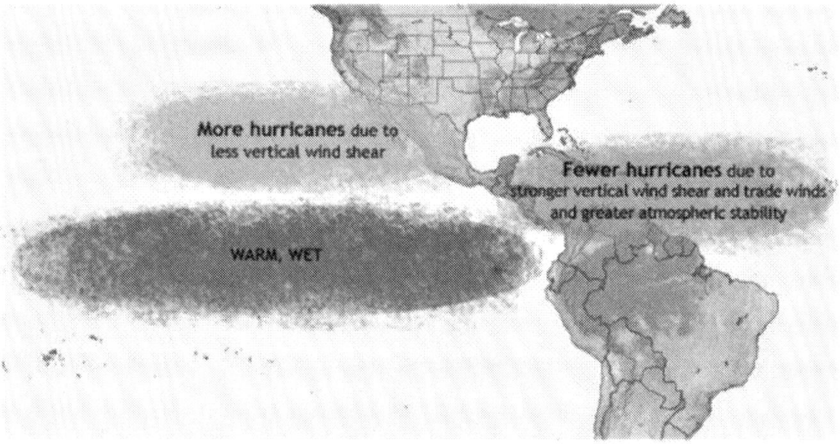

Impact of El Niño on hurricanes
Source: NOAA climate.gov, based on originals by Gerry Bell

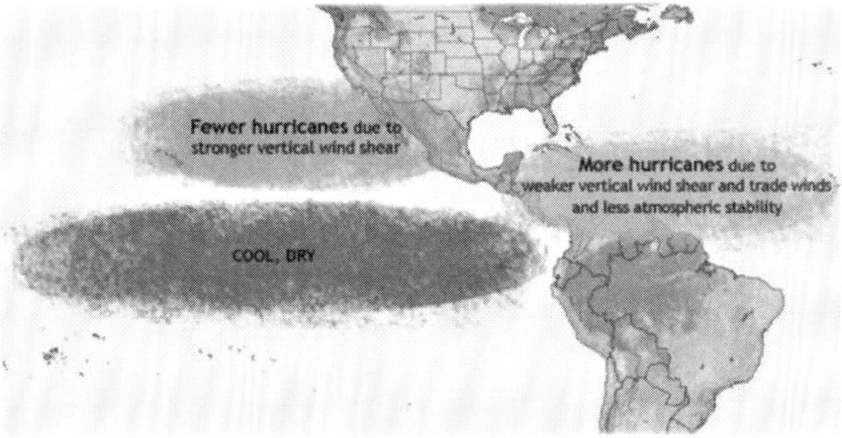

Impact of La Niña on hurricanes
Source: NOAA climate.gov, based on originals by Gerry Bell

SJ:
On the north coast of Cuba, based on my research in the 1770s, when we find an El Niño year, that is the drought phase in the Caribbean, we can show drought conditions affected the cattle ranching, and people writing in the local records about the *peste*, or a disease that affected the cattle. Cattle was the major agricultural product at that time. The subsequent La Niña phase sent massive flooding into the valleys around the towns.

This was a period in which the state began to show an interest in dealing with the outcomes of such natural phenomena, rather than simply leaving the response to local initiatives.

SJ:
It's clear that the authorities were learning from their mistakes, and mandating a rapid government response. In the 1750s, the people in charge were the church. By the mid-1760s, the government had taken the initiative to mandate that their people go around immediately after the hurricane and begin assessing the damage, and taking measures to remedy the situation. They also took measures to get food. And they recognise that they were in a crisis situation, and allowed merchants to go to different colonies and get emergency supplies, increasingly relaxing these regulations.

The alternation of storm and drought continues to be reflected in the local chronicles throughout the nineteenth century. But now, for the first time, actual hurricanes are identified. The century opened in 1800 with a year of smallpox and storms; with subsequent hurricanes recorded in 1812, 1821, 1826, 1831, 1832 and 1835. In 1837, for the first time a local storm is actually named: that of 'San Evaristo'.

By this time, sugar was quickly becoming Cuba's primary product – and sugar plantations were slowly developing in the Caibarién area. These proved to be particularly susceptible to the impact of large storms.

LER:
The cane fields were particularly vulnerable to the impact of the wind. The sugar cane falls, it is practically knocked to the ground, and that makes the task of cutting harder, requiring greater effort, and much of the cane is lost.

The sugar that had already been produced, packaged firstly in boxes and afterwards in sacks, was often completely lost, when the places where these boxes and sacks of sugar were deposited became flooded or made damp by the rain. And this would lead to an enormous amount of loss.

The same occurred when the railways began to be developed, and with that the possibility of transporting sugar production, and agricultural production in general, towards the ports situated on the coasts. The sea surges often razed the port installations, with the docks and the warehouses where these commodities were deposited for their subsequent embarkation towards the United States and Europe. So, the losses caused by the hurricanes were always plentiful, on land as well as at sea.

However, sugar estates were able to recover quickly. While a season's crop might be damaged, this could readily be overcome (and much of the crop still made use of), and production restored in time for the next season.

HV:
With sugar, there was always the capacity to recover, because it was a highly valued commodity.

This was not the case with what had been, up until then, a very important crop for Cuba: coffee. Unlike sugarcane, coffee trees took several years to reach maturity, and so it was much harder for coffee estates to recover from the damage a hurricane might cause. This seems to have been particularly significant when in the 1840s a series of severe hurricanes in quick succession hit western Cuba.

LER:
Western Cuba came to have large coffee plantations, towards the middle of the nineteenth century, but following the impact of two important hurricanes in 1844 and 1846, these coffee plantations never recovered nor returned to the splendour that they had previously.

RF:
The hurricanes of 1844 and 1846 affected many of the coffee estates that were to the south of Havana, as well as in what is now the Sierra del Rosario.

OZ:
That hurricane, in 1846, practically came to be the tombstone for these plantations, because it destroyed many of them, and there was no economic sense in working for their recovery. While they were operating with existing coffee trees, the costs were low. But to replant, to remake the plantations at a time when the market for Cuban coffee had collapsed – there was no economic benefit. So, the plantations were simply abandoned, and in many cases the land was occupied by cane.

SJ:
The hurricanes in the nineteenth century had a dramatic impact. In terms of cultivation of sugarcane, it advanced sugarcane production because it destroyed the competition crops, especially coffee. Three successive hurricanes in the 1840s virtually wiped out the coffee industry. And the conclusion is that the slaves who were working in the coffee industry were sold into the sugar industry, which recovered quicker from these extreme events than the coffee could recover.

But it is important not to overstate the significance of hurricanes – important though they of course were in the life of the island. Although these meteorological events may have helped hasten the decline of the Cuban coffee industry, they were by no means the only cause.

RF:
Many factors interacted and explain why the Cuban economy increasingly specialised in sugar, rather than other crops. I would say that the hurricanes were just one of the factors, and not the determining factor for the decline of Cuban coffee. It had more to do with the rise of Brazilian coffee. Brazil rapidly became the largest exporter, with large plantations that were more similar to the sugar plantations in Cuba, rather than the late-eighteenth century coffee plantations in Haiti, or in the early-nineteenth century in Cuba.

OZ:
Without doubt, the decline of coffee had several factors. There were the natural conditions in Cuba for intense and competitive coffee cultivation. It had been able to become established in the first decades of the nineteenth century, until Brazil appeared with all its potential. And then there was the commercial situation. That is, the US, which was the principal market for Cuban coffee, enforced punishing customs duties against Spain, and raised the tariff on Cuban coffee. Neither in quality nor in price could it compete with Brazilian coffee in the North American market from the 1830s.

RF:
There were also environmental causes of the decline. These plantations lasted twenty, thirty years, and then they declined. The soil lost its fertility. The erosion of these hills also intensified, along with that process.

Nevertheless, it is clear that the hurricanes of the 1840s, coming as they did in such quick succession and in particular affecting the most important agricultural areas of Cuba, had at least a catalytic impact on the direction that Cuba's rural economy would take over the coming decades.

Reconstructed coffee estate, Sierra del Rosario, Cuba (2019)
Photo: Gonzalo Vidal

OZ:
In the midst of this, there is a hurricane which even if it didn't bring about the disappearance of coffee, did reinforce its decline in western Cuba, apart from in some places towards Pinar del Río, in the Sierra de los Órganos. It was a mortal blow for the coffee plantations in the West, and above all in the jurisdiction around Havana.

RF:
The hurricanes obviously have an influence, because it takes longer for coffee to recover, probably, than was the case of sugar or other crops. But I would say that it wasn't the principal factor. It was a factor that influenced this process a lot, but I think that it was going to happen anyway. After the 1840s, 1850s, Cuba didn't have an important role in the world coffee market. In the eastern zone coffee production lasted longer. In reality what Cuba had after this era was small coffee plantations. Never the large slave plantations like those seen in Brazil.

Tobacco was the other important Cuban crop, and this also suffered the effects of extreme weather.

> *SJ:*
> We've also seen evidence in tobacco-producing areas that sequential bad weather is very detrimental to the tobacco producing, and by the mid-1860s, tobacco was again in crisis.
>
> *LER:*
> In the case of tobacco, principally focused on the western region and centre of the country in the nineteenth century, this was also badly damaged and destroyed. Not just the plants that were still growing in the soil, but also the harvested tobacco in the drying barns.

Of course, all areas of the economy could be harmed, at least in the short term, by a particularly strong storm.

> *LER:*
> I should also mention the significance of hurricanes for colliers, those who manufacture charcoal, and fishermen. The people who fabricated coal in ovens, and those fishermen who in a practically isolated fashion fished on the small islands that ring the Cuban archipelago. Often, they didn't even know that a hurricane was approaching Cuban territory, and they were simply exterminated by the force of the sea and the winds.

This was something that the inhabitants of Caibarién – many of whom fished in the waters around the nearby keys – were very familiar with. The local chronicle for Caibarién continued to list the prominent storms that occurred throughout the nineteenth century, with notable hurricanes in 1870, 1876 and 1882. But it was the hurricane of 4th September 1888 that figured particularly strongly in popular memory in the local region.

> *OZ:*
> The hurricane affected an area that was economically developed. That is, the area of Yaguajay was still being established, and towards Placetas as well, but the sugar industry was already well implanted in the region.

Tracks of September and October 1876 hurricanes
Map courtesty of Luis Enrique Ramos

> *MN:*
> I can tell you an anecdote. My mother – who is still alive, going on 93 years old – had a grandmother who grew up on the keys. In the hurricane of 1888, she was the only one who survived the enormous waves that caused a storm surge, along with the force of the hurricane. Her and a goat. They saved themselves by floating on top of a table. Well, my whole lineage comes from that.

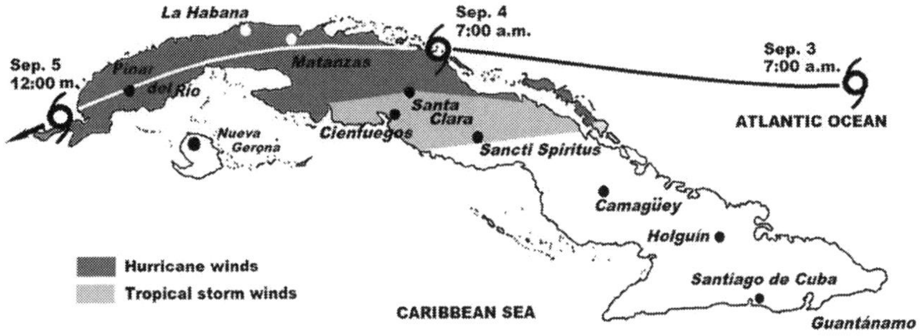

Track of 1888 hurricane
Map courtesty of Luis Enrique Ramos

The hurricane on 23rd September 1894 also had a local impact on Caibarién. While serious flooding was experienced further up the coast, in Sagua, sailors from Caibarién were amongst those who went to help with the rescue effort.

It was clear that the more developed the Cuban economy and its infrastructure became, the greater the cost of hurricanes when they hit.

LER:
With the development of industry, hurricanes caused a lot more damage in economic terms – when the industrial installations, and the networks for electricity, telephones and public lighting, ended up destroyed by a hurricane. The north of what became Las Villas [now Villa Clara] province, and which used to be the Central Department of the island, is a region that historically has maintained a wealth in sugar. As a result, the losses both in cane that was being cultivated and in the industries that processed this sugarcane in order to extract its products, were frequently devastating. So, we have several hurricanes that were significant because of the damage they caused. For example, the large hurricanes of 1888, 1894, 1919, 1933, 1985 (Hurricane Kate), and most recently Hurricane Irma. All of these swept the north-central coast of Cuba, and caused enormous losses valued in many cases in millions of pesos.

Going into the twentieth century, the 1930s proved to be a particularly active decade for hurricanes, with three having a notable local impact in Caibarién. Of these, the so-called 'Hurricane of Santa Cruz del Sur', of 1932, was the deadliest to ever hit Cuba. A Category 5 storm, like Irma, it crossed the centre of the island, causing over three thousand deaths. Although the Caibarién area was spared the worst, with the brunt being borne by the town of Santa Cruz del Sur, on the southern coast – which was all but obliterated by a storm surge bringing 6.5 metre-high waves, and where most of the deaths were caused – its ravages were felt on the north coast as well.

The Cuba-Brownsville hurricane of 1933 was another Category 5 storm. Of the 17 Cuban sugar mills in its path, 7 were heavily damaged, and 5 were destroyed; while the ports along the northern coast, including Caibarién, suffered significant harm. Around six hundred boats were sunk, and 185 people were killed.

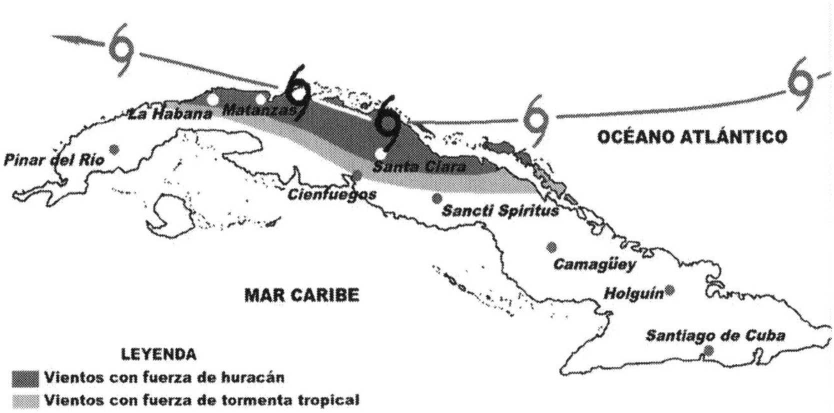

Track of 1933 hurricane
Map courtesty of Luis Enrique Ramos

LER:
In 1933, the losses caused by the hurricane of August/September of that year, ten million dollars were lost in the island, and it needs to be seen what ten million dollars signified in 1933 compared to the exchange value now [approximately 200 million dollars, at 2020 prices].

MN:
During the 1933 hurricane, the sea penetrated Caibarién. Quite a few warehouses were destroyed. Our town had an extensive network of warehouses, and many owners of these saw them destroyed by the force of the waters and winds. The sea penetrated as far as what are now Falero and Jiménez streets. My mother and her family, my grandmother, lost everything because the water reached higher than a person, and the few resources that they had then (this was the era of Machado), well, they lost them. The mattresses, the sewing machine, they practically lost everything. Above all the fishermen were affected, who were used to living on the seafront, in one of the poorest settlements that we had.

The 1933 hurricane was unusual in that there appeared to be a direct connection with significant political events in Cuba.

LER:
It isn't frequent that hurricanes have a specific effect on the historical events that mark the great moments of Cuban history, because hurricanes, from a time perspective, are brief. They occur over two or three days, and would have to coincide with a very significant event for the hurricane to produce a change. Nevertheless, this did occur in the case of the hurricane that affected the central part of Cuba in 1933, when the dictator Gerardo Machado had recently been forced by the people to flee the country. After the hurricane crossed Cuba between 30th August and 1st September, the then provisional President of the Republic, Carlos Manuel de Céspedes, decided to visit the zones that had been devastated, in the north of Las Villas province. On leaving Havana, the centre of power, this president who had still not consolidated his power and his government, left a power vacuum. This was taken advantage of by a group of low-ranking army officers, led by a sergeant called Fulgencio Batista, who would come to have a disastrous impact on Cuban history. Utilising this power vacuum, they assumed the government in Havana through an insurrection and coup d'état. They deposed that president who had still not consolidated his control, Carlos Manuel de Céspedes, and took over the government of the country.

Damage caused to sugar mill by 1933 hurricane
Photo courtesy of Luis Enrique Ramos

Damage caused by 1933 hurricane
Photos courtesy of Luis Enrique Ramos

While the large hurricane that hit Havana in October 1944 crossed the island too far west to have a serious impact on the Caibarién area, 1952's Hurricane Fox passed right over the town.

> *MN:*
> There were wind gusts of 200 kph here in Caibarién, according to the measurements collected by the history of the meteorological station, which is one of the oldest stations in Cuba.

Fox produced very substantial rainfall over the central region of Cuba, and there was a great deal of flooding as rivers overflowed. A total of 600 people were killed in the island, and the damages included 36 of Cuba's 261 sugar mills, with the winds causing the destruction of many buildings.

For many of today's residents of Caibarién, Hurricane Flora in 1963 marks the earliest cyclonic memory – as it does for the country as a whole. It came in the midst of the tumultuous initial years following the 1959 revolution, and was the subject of Santiago Alvarez's film *Ciclón*, which documented the proactive popular response to a storm that, more than any other, took on a character of its own. While most hurricanes arrive, and continue their trajectory, Flora was different. It sat over the eastern

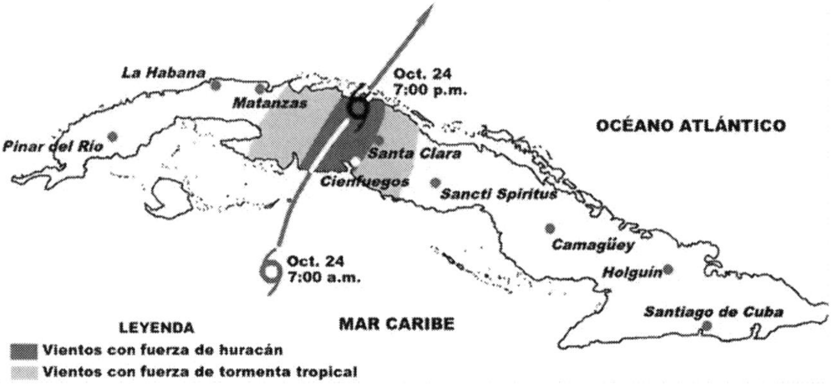

Track of Hurricane Fox (1952)
Map courtesty of Luis Enrique Ramos

half of Cuba, slowly meandering backwards and forwards for several days before finally departing. As a result, vast quantities of water were dumped on the island, causing very extensive flooding; and a total of 1,750 people died, with an estimated half-a-billion dollars' worth of physical damage. As Alvarez's documentary said:

> The hurricane that battered the country has caused considerable loss of human life and great destruction. During six consecutive days the people of the eastern provinces have fought a painful and valiant struggle against the furious hurricane, and the unprecedented floods it brought with it.

PG:
When I was a boy, I remember having prepared for Hurricane Flora, which was erratic, and when it left the east of Cuba headed towards the central region, and then withdrew. We moved into my grandparents' house, arriving on the morning that Flora was going to hit us. It had already been hitting Cuba for a week.

However, for the inhabitants of Caibarién, 1985's Hurricane Kate is now their point of reference, against which the more recent Irma is compared.

PG:
Until Hurricane Kate in 1985, there were small cyclones, but never a large hurricane. Then Kate was a Category 2, and when it reached Caibarién it was Category 1.

AAG:
It followed a period in which Cuba had lived through a kind of psychological truce. There had been hurricanes, but they had passed us by, and so we had lost something of the perception of danger.

Coming as it did so late in the hurricane season, and following a relatively quiet period in Cuba in terms of cyclonic activity, Kate came as something of a surprise.

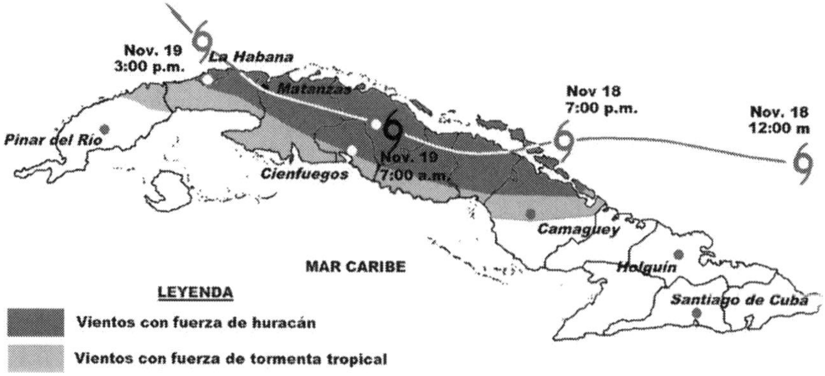

Track of Hurricane Kate (1985)
Map courtesy of Luis Enrique Ramos

AAG:
The hurricane came from Puerto Rico, if I remember correctly. There was a line of storms and weak winds in the north, and a kind of heightened temperature. If I remember right, it entered between Ciego de Ávila and Caibarién on the 19th November. There was a horrendous storm. I have lived through many hurricanes, but I had never seen the eye of a hurricane. And I experienced the eye of Hurricane Kate. You know that a hurricane has three fundamental parts: the cloud band, the eye and the wall of the eye, where the strongest winds are. I have experienced the cloud band and the edge of hurricanes many times. In Cuba, everyone has seen them. But the eye with its wall – only when Kate passed through Caibarién.

PG:
What's interesting about Kate was the complete lack of information. They didn't evacuate many people, because they weren't expecting it to arrive so soon.

AC:
At the time of Hurricane Kate in 1985, there wasn't the same level of development at the Institute of Meteorology and internationally as there is today. There weren't the satellites we have today, there weren't the observational methods we have today.

Despite the local perception of official inaction, some three hundred thousand people were evacuated along the length of the country as Kate progressed – including from Caibarién. This no doubt helped to ensure that there were no fatalities in Cuba.

AAG:
Almost a thousand people were evacuated [from Caibarién]. In Kate, nobody died, and in Irma neither.

Official warnings were issued. But it seems that there was a feeling of complacency in the population, grown somewhat unused to such storms.

AAG:
When Kate came, I remember that, despite the warnings given by the Institute of Meteorology, the town didn't have a perception of the danger. I remember my mother had gone to work at the biscuit factory. She has always been afraid of the winds, and when she found out that the hurricane was coming, she mentioned it to her workmates. They said, 'And this foolishness? We'll stay here. I don't think it's coming close.' The factory worked normally. They didn't take any measures to reinforce it. They left at four or five in the afternoon, and at seven that night you could feel the gusts.

Like Irma, Kate hit Caibarién during the night. No doubt this intensified the experience and impression that it left on the town's inhabitants.

PG:
It arrived in the early hours of the morning. I remember that my mother woke me and my wife up. She told me, come into the house because you're living in a shack and it's going to collapse.

AAG:
I was in bed, but I remember that through the window it became very dark, so dark. The atmosphere heavy. That's when the eye came past. We felt the hurricane-force winds. You could hear the noise of the wind, it was impressive. I got up as best I could, and went to the window, and saw the spectacle. We had never seen the eye, nor did we realise the danger, there was no direct conception of the danger.

AAG:
I remember how the wind bent the plants. How the trees fell, and how the electric cables broke. And how the branches flew, and the cans flew, and the rubbish bins flew. They hadn't been collected. They hadn't cut the few trees that there were. No measures had been taken. Although some people were evacuated.

PG:
We were living two hundred metres from the sea. We lived in a street very close to the sea, which was distressing. Seeing the sea come in, during the night.

AAG:
I remember that when the eye passed, everyone went out into the street, because after a tremendously strong gust there came an absolute calm, but it was a ghostly calm. I remember that I went out as well, with the help of crutches, and you could see the stars. And there was a silence that contrasted with the enormous noise the hurricane was making before. And suddenly, a calm, but a heavy calm. It was a calm you could touch. There was something unreal. Afterwards I learned that this was the low pressure. We were passing through the centre of the hurricane, which is characterised by low pressure, naturally. And the low pressure creates this strange sensation, like a demolishing of reality. The word spread: we have to quickly get back inside, because it's going to come back even stronger. Afterwards the winds were as strong, or even stronger than the first part of the wall. And the hurricane could be felt throughout the night.

PG:
We found out that the sea was rising when we saw it covering the floor. In my house it didn't rise much, because we lived in a zone that was fairly high. But the adjacent houses, they all lost fridges, mattresses, electrical goods, everything.

AAG:
The following morning, it had left Caibarién. And I told my brother to take me by bicycle, because I couldn't walk, and I wanted to see. Our block was horrific. The streets. The sea penetrated to four hundred metres. The boats that couldn't be protected were floating in the middle of the street. The roofs fallen, and the electric cables.

Damage caused by Hurricane Kate, Playa Uvero, Villa Clara (1985)
Photo courtesy of Wilder Llanes Méndez

The few trees that Caibarién had were on the ground. The people complaining. They were taking the damp mattresses out into the sun. There were fridges and televisions floating on the sea. Many electric appliances were lost. The cables were on the ground, the roofs collapsed, the glass smashed from the shop windows, bits of zinc everywhere. A lot of seaweed from the sea covered the streets, and gave a salty smell. Furniture brought out to dry, and towels and clothes.

PG:
We woke on 20th November 1985 to find the town devastated. People were on the roofs of the houses, because the sea had flooded them, and the water hadn't withdrawn yet. The flooding was severe. That was what was worst, the flooding by the sea, because the sea is unrelenting. We don't have floods because of fresh rainwater, which besides is less damaging than a flood of salt water, which destroys everything it touches. For example, the mattresses don't recover after being soaked by salt water. If they get wet from fresh water, you can put them out to dry, and they can recuperate. The salt water oxidises tools, and all electrical equipment collapses because it becomes choked by the salt and cannot be repaired. It was a complete disaster for the city.

AAG:
The people didn't shout, they didn't cry, but you could feel the weight of the hurricane in their looks, in their gestures. The destruction. I don't remember anybody crying. No human lives were lost. But you could feel the disaster. The disaster was great.

AM:
Kate caused a lot of damage. Because of the poor, weak residential infrastructure that there was at that time in Cuba, now 34 years ago, the damage was very severe. But as a hurricane, Kate was less than half of Irma. It was a Category 2 hurricane, which doesn't have the same impact. The sea came in a lot more, due to us not having the sea wall of the Malecón – which is practically a dyke. It even won a prize, a certificate for being one of the best protective works in Cuba for maritime impacts in Caibarién, which is considered to be amongst the municipalities on the north coast of Cuba suffering most from the effects of the sea, from the waves hitting.

Sea wall (Malecón), Caibarién (2019)
Photo: Gonzalo Vidal

PG:
The impact of Kate was much more serious [than Irma] because of the damage caused to the residential infrastructure, because of the tide and everything else. The sea came in much more than it did with Irma. The damage caused by Kate stems from the lack of previous preparation in the population. Nobody was prepared for that.

In addition to the considerable impact that Kate had on housing in coastal communities such as Caibarién, it had a particularly devastating effect on important sectors of the economy. Arriving as it did close to the start of the main sugar-harvesting season, it caused substantial damage to that year's crop. Almost ten thousand square kilometres of cane were destroyed, along with 37,000 tons of already-processed sugar. Other produce was also affected – bananas in particular, as well as other fruits and vegetables.

AAG:
A lot of sugar was lost, because there wasn't time to save it. A large banana plantation that Caibarién had was lost, and also many sugar plantations. Many cane fields were lost. And the lobster company suffered a lot of damage. There was a power cut that lasted four days. I remember that the municipal government took the decision to sell to the population the already processed lobster that was in the cold storage, because the cold storage didn't have any electricity to function and so they decided to sell it to the people at modest prices. Also many popular provision stores were damaged by the wind, and the food was going bad. The factory where my parents worked lost the whole of its roof, because they didn't take any measures, which they should have done – despite the warnings that were made. They had no conception of the danger.

PG:
I think that after Kate we were ten days without electricity. Or perhaps a lot less. Because Hurricane Kate did not have very strong winds, though there was a lot of water. It rained, but it didn't knock down the posts, and it didn't damage the electrical infrastructure, which besides had been recently renovated.

MN:
Hurricanes have always caused a lot of damage in Caibarién, above all along the seafront, because of the economic characteristics of the population living there, as their houses were too weak to withstand the attacks of the hurricanes.

RR:
In a way, Kate prepared us, because afterwards the houses were strengthened. Those that were on the seafront had been made of wood, but now they are built from brick. And this made us stronger when Irma came.

Certainly hurricanes have always been a fact of life in Caibarién, and Cuba as a whole, coming with varying degrees of intensity. While some periods see heightened activity, during others the danger appears to recede. However, such times often bring the less spectacular, but at least as devastating, droughts that cause a longer lasting impact on agriculture. But the perception is that in recent years, the intensity and frequency appears to be on the increase.

AC:
After 1995, we find ourselves in an active period. These are natural cycles. But it needs to be stressed, it seems that in recent years there has been an intensification. In a short period of time, hurricanes have been arriving with greater intensity. There has been a clear increase in the number of intense hurricanes that have touched land. This has been observed.

LER:
When talking about hurricanes, it is perhaps of interest to note that although there is no evidence that the total number of hurricanes has increased in recent years, it seems that the number of high intensity hurricanes compared with this total has possibly been increasing. It needs to be determined whether this is a statistically significant increase, or if it is a tendency that afterwards will disappear. Nevertheless, this doesn't affect at all the need to guarantee protective measures against the danger, the vulnerabilities and the risks, because over and above one cause or another, of the magnitude of one cause or another, the danger, vulnerability and risk continue to be present.

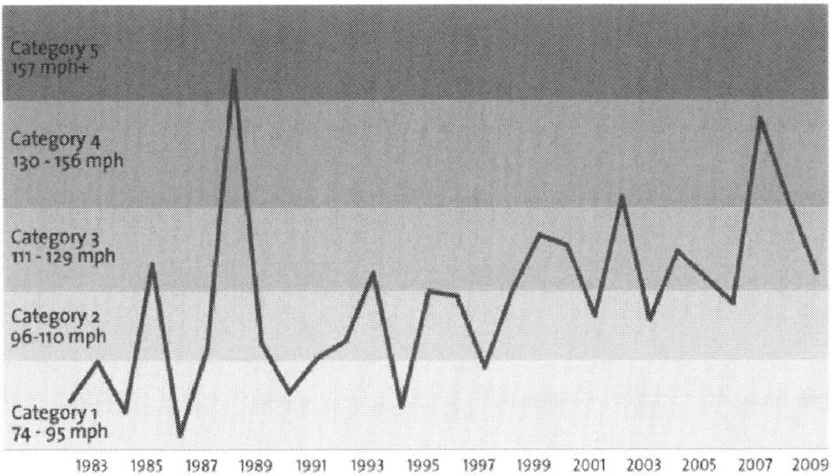

The rising strength of North Atlantic hurricanes (1983-2009)
Source: Jim Kossin, National Climate Data Center

AC:
Hurricanes are becoming more intense because there is a greater warming of the Earth's surface in the tropical belts, middle latitudes, and in fact the ocean. So it seems to us that in part global warming and the so called climate change may very well be associated with a more rapid intensification of a hurricane, an increase in the number of intense hurricanes, and also what we have seen in Cuba.

Here, in studies from 25 to 30 years ago, the intense hurricanes were almost exclusively in the western half of Cuba. And in the last 13 years, we have seen a change in behaviour of the trajectories over Cuba. For example, the eastern region of Cuba has been, you could say, impacted by intense hurricanes. For example: Hurricane Dennis in July 2005, in Veracruz, Category 4; Hurricane Ike, Punta Lucrecia, Holguin Province, 2008; Hurricane Sandy, Santiago de Cuba, Category 3, 2012. The hurricane that affected the Baracoa area, the Guantánamo region, was a very intense hurricane. It seems evident that the intense hurricanes that before were more exclusive to the western part of the island, to the centre, have displaced towards the eastern region. And it has to be said that Irma was the first Category 5 hurricane to touch the north coast of Cuba since records began in 1850.

AAG:
Thanks to my work, for almost seven years I had to travel the whole length of the country, and I could see the disasters. Days after Matthew hit Baracoa [2016], Sandy in Santiago de Cuba [2012], Ike and Gustav in Pinar del Rio [2008]. Ike and Gustav passed with just days between them. The eye passed through Viñales. Imagine it, those two eyes passed with barely a fortnight between them. Those were days in which you could see the devastation of the vegetation was enormous.

In Caibarién we didn't see much of that with Kate, because Caibarién didn't have many trees. But, for example, in Santiago de Cuba, when Sandy passed, and Viñales with Ike and Gustav, what had the most impact on me was how the vegetation was spoiled. It looked like another landscape. It looked like another world. We saw things that hadn't been seen before. They hadn't been seen, because they were covered by the vegetation. Houses that you didn't know were there. It gave the impression of living in another town. In Santiago de Cuba, I stayed in the Hotel Santiago. I saw a city that grew from amongst the trees. It gave the impression that Santiago was a forest in which houses had been built. After Sandy passed, it gave the impression that there were some trees growing from within the city, and you could see houses that I had never seen before.

I never had that impression with Kate. But I did with Sandy. And Matthew, when it passed through Baracoa. I visited a week later, and the disaster was immense. Worse than what I saw with Kate. And the vegetation, which is lush there, seemed like somewhere out of hell, a place where almost all the palms had been decapitated. The trees ripped up by their roots. The houses without roofs. I remember that from there we went by boat along the River Toa, which is a fast-flowing river, the fastest flowing in Cuba, and along its length it had lost metres of its bank, because of the strength of the waters that came down.

LER:
The impact of hurricanes is affected by the rising sea level, alongside which the height of the waves increases as well. If we overlap this with modification of coasts, wind speed, and even a factor that is often not taken into account, which is the astronomical tides, it can give rise to phenomena of unusual severity.

In the centre of Cuba there is an area that is particularly vulnerable, which is the coastal zone – the whole of the north coast. Cuba, which is a country with more than five thousand kilometres of coast, has a great many places where there is a risk of flooding due to hurricanes. In fact, if we historically analyse the behaviour of these phenomena in Cuba, there are sixteen coastal localities that in the last hundred years have suffered at least three floods due to hurricanes. And three of these are situated on the north coast of Cuba's central region. These are Caibarién, Isabela de Sagua (which gives Sagua la Grande access to the sea), and Cárdenas – which is in the province of Matanzas, but we should also see as being part of this geographic zone.

The case of Irma shows that in recent years, it seems that there has been a tendency not towards an increase in the total number of hurricanes, but perhaps in the number of intense hurricanes. If we take into account that the north coast of the central region of Cuba is situated on the south side of the Gulf Stream – which is a river of warm water, that constitutes a source of fuel, you might say, for hurricanes – so we should make a historical analysis of the passage of Irma over the centre of the country, and see it as reason for alarm. It should become an experience that informs what future actions the communities that are situated in that region must adopt in order to prepare for the repetition of such phenomena.

3 Living with Hurricanes

When we live in a context in which there are all these events around us, the only way to come out of it as unaffected as possible is through preparation. And preparation comes from knowledge. If I don't know about the phenomenon, or how to face up to the possibility that it might give me a bad time, then that is a problem. When I know the characteristics of what I am confronting, then I can be better prepared.

Manuel Iturralde-Vinent

Although it can never be known exactly when or where a hurricane is going to arrive, for a country such as Cuba they are a historic certainty. That being the case, not only is it necessary to develop appropriate approaches for mitigating their impact and dealing with their aftermath, but also to learn how to live with their ever-present threat.

SJ:
When historians think about how disaster management or disaster response has evolved over a very long period, over centuries, it's clear that we are beginning to see different periods emerging.

In recent years Cuba has earned a well-deserved reputation for its effective and rapid response to potential disasters such as hurricanes. This has been facilitated by there being – since the 1959 revolution – a strong, interventionist state, organised at every level from the national down to the local, that sees it as being its responsibility to deal with such occurrences. It is interesting to note that historically this is not the first time that the island has had such an official response.

> *SJ:*
> Before roughly the mid-eighteenth century, that is before the Enlightenment began to spread, disaster response was primarily in the hands of the Catholic church. The church, the parish priests, knew its parishioners best, and it knew when people were missing. It knew what houses were destroyed, it knew how to effectively manage the resources that it could muster, or it could accumulate. With the advent of the Enlightenment, however, and the arrival of absolute monarchy, the metropolitan governments began to take a much greater role, or a more active role, a more involved role in the idea of disaster response. In the case of the Spaniards they sent orders to the local authorities to begin taking stock, to be reporting back to the Captain General in Havana. The Captain General in Havana sent out laws for the collection of things like palm thatch, which Cubans call '*guano*', to re-roof houses. It required, for example, people to provide food, *platanos* [bananas], which were the first food that would be destroyed, but the first that could be picked up from the ground. It also surprisingly passed laws against price gouging. There were severe penalties for price gouging.

However, from the end of the eighteenth century the tendency turned more towards voluntaristic responses, somewhat more haphazard in their effectiveness at dealing with the storms when they struck.

> *SJ:*
> By the time of the American Independence period, that is 1776, and the idea of the rights of man, John Locke, and especially individualism, the idea of disaster response passed from an intrusive metropolitan Spanish government into an idea that the individual was responsible for their own welfare. The state gradually took a backseat. But when disasters happen – for example, after 1870 – historians can discern the rise of the involvement of voluntary organisations and especially the Red Cross.

This approach to disaster response required the call for, at a local level, churches, community organisations, fraternal organisations, to enlist their members to send donations, which would be sent to the central organisation, and then distributed to relief organisations. This approach lasted well into the twentieth century.

At the beginning of the second half of the twentieth century, once again the government began to take a much more active role in the response to hurricanes, and who should be responsible for providing the relief supplies necessary, and the distribution and organisation when they were on the ground.

Paramount for being able to effectively deal with hurricanes and their consequences is having sufficient knowledge of weather conditions to be able to develop early-warning mechanisms, which might permit the taking of appropriate action to limit the storm's impact – and reduce if not the amount of material damage caused, at least the loss to human life. This required the development of the science of meteorology.

MN:
In times past, there was a lack of scientific knowledge, and social preparation to overcome the effects of hurricanes was deficient. Meteorology has become effective with the development of science and technology, locally and globally.

In Cuba, although since the earliest times observation was being made of the passing of hurricanes – after all, they were spectacularly difficult to miss – it was in 1858 that meteorological studies really began there. In that year, a meteorological observatory was established at the Belen College in Havana, which began taking regular readings of atmospheric pressure, temperature and cloud conditions. Study of cyclonic events as such became systematised after 1870, with the arrival from France of Benito Viñes. Although lacking equipment more sophisticated than a thermometer and barometer, he made precise measurements of cloud movements as hurricanes approached. By 1880, Cuba was issuing warnings about approaching storms.

Following independence, the Cuban government founded a state observatory in 1908, and gradually a network of weather stations was established

Colegio de Belén, Havana, Cuba (1950s)
Source: Wikipedia

across the island, centralising their readings. By the 1940s, eleven such stations were operational – including one at Caibarién.

> *MN:*
> Caibarién's meteorological station is one of the oldest in the country. It was founded in the 1930s. It was one of the approximately seventeen that were in place in 1959. One of the eleven that remained in 1963. Now there are sixty-eight stations, and eight meteorological radars that monitor the weather in our country.

From the 1950s, these were able to coordinate with and complement the weather-studying aeroplanes of the National Hurricane Center in Miami, and the World Meteorological Organisation.

> *AC:*
> In the 1960s, the satellite era began, and now we have satellites with high resolution. So now we see more than we could before. Before there was no way of knowing if there was a hurricane in the Atlantic, unless ships reported it. Now there are better methods of detection, better techniques, better tools, and today we see more than we saw before.

Meteorological Station, Caibarién
Source: Centro Meteorológico Provincial de Villa Clara

Satellite image showing Hurricanes Irma, José and Katia (September 2017)
Source: National Oceanic and Atmospheric Administration

Although the Cuban state had already been concerning itself with the development of meteorological forecasts, following the 1959 revolution the government became a lot more proactive in its efforts aimed at limiting the impact that hurricanes, and other such natural phenomena, might have.

LER:
Of course, hurricanes can cause damage in any country, in any territory. And that doesn't exactly have anything to do with the socio-economic or political system that the country might have. Nevertheless, we should say that after 1959, after the triumph of the revolution, in Cuba a very interesting process began, which is that the state began to take a lot more responsibility over the lives of citizens and the preservation of material wealth that was put in danger by any hurricane that approached Cuban territory.

For this, three very important institutions were established. First, Civil Defence, which is the organisation that coordinates the prevention operations, confronting hurricanes as natural disasters. It concerns itself with foreseeing what measures of precaution need to be taken by the population; what needs to be mobilised in order to evacuate those who are in dangerous locations; and directs recovery operations after the hurricane has passed.

Second, the National Meteorological Service, which was strengthened with the creation of the Institute of Meteorology in 1965, which now can count on 68 meteorological stations and 8 radars. These permit coverage of the whole of the national territory, and provide greater scientific support for quality weather forecasts, both as to the trajectory and the intensity of the hurricanes.

And third, the Institute of Hydraulic Resources, which built a great number of installations such as dams, channels and reservoirs, which are destined in the first place for the storing of water when it rains to guarantee a reserve that can be utilised when there are periods of less rain, in periods of drought. But at the same time, they can help stop or at least slow down the development of flooding, when there is a hurricane that generates very abundant rain.

This infrastructure, covering the entire island, has enabled Cuba to be forewarned and well-prepared for any impending meteorological event that might occur. To this has been added a quite impressive level of social

Institute of Meteorology and Observatory, Casablanca, Havana
Source: Instituto de Meteorología de Cuba

organisation, that permits the country to respond with great speed and effectiveness so as to mitigate, as much as is possible, any possible negative impact.

LER:
These are complemented by the national public health system, and above all with the regional governmental structures that are established from the base up, with the smallest territories that we call 'Popular Councils' (*Consejo Popular*). And these structures themselves have centres for the management of natural disasters, which integrate all the social forces and state institutions in seeking to detain as much as possible, and reduce the impact of these disasters. These are also replicated in the municipalities, provinces and at the national level, known as 'Defence Councils' (*Consejos de Defensa*).

So it is a well thought-out system, building on the experience obtained; and it has demonstrated on more than one occasion, with ten intense hurricanes in recent years hitting Cuba, that this system effectively succeeds in reducing to a minimum the loss of life, whenever a hurricane affects a particular region.

AF:
Concerning the impact of extreme events, I believe that Cuba has the correct policy, which has been functioning until now, and which has the peculiarity of the existence of very flexible mechanisms that convert the local government, in moments of risk, into an element in which Civil Defence and all the political and economic factors in the territory come together, in order to prevent any possible disaster. The people are evacuated. Each municipality even has its own protocol, and determines who is at risk. In the case of a hurricane, for example, they know what to do. That is, first it is necessary to protect life. Second, protect every part of the economy. Prevent the loss not only of the local economic capital of the territory, but also of its people.

An important element of this is keeping the general population well-informed as to what is happening – at least meteorologically – and what measures should be taken to weather the storm.

AC:
The information is given in the normal television studio. The danger is spoken about. The need to be prepared is spoken about, and the need to attentively follow the information given by National Defence. The hurricane warnings are given by our Forecast Centre at the Institute of Meteorology. And then when there is a potential danger, measures are dictated, on the radio or in the printed press. The media takes responsibility for passing on to the population a whole series of measures. Measures resulting from the hurricane now constituting a threat, moving from being a potential to an imminent threat. 'Imminent' generally means within 24 or 36 hours.

The measures taken ensure that when it is known that a hurricane is going to impact a particular region directly, tropical cyclone warnings are transmitted when it is known that there is a real threat. This is known with some precision about 24 to 36 hours beforehand, although sometimes we can be certain with three-days' warning that the hurricane is going to touch Cuba. But we can never say with that amount of anticipation the exact point where the centre of the hurricane will penetrate, because what the numeric models do is make a simulation. Generally, one must interpret four simulations daily. For example, simulations are made at 2pm, at 8pm, at 2am and at 8am. These are four versions of the model that have to be evaluated and compared. There might be differences, so what has to be seen are the averages of the oscillations for the likely location at each hour.

PG:
The warning system has improved a lot, obviously. They simply prepare better now. There is also a process of preparation for earthquakes, because they can predict what zone is going to shake. Not with the same anticipation as a hurricane, but there are means for foreseeing that something is going to happen with the tectonic faults.

AC:
I've been working for 35 years, and I've seen a transition from classic synoptic meteorology, to cyber-meteorology, a computerised meteorology, like in medicine. The technological advances have been incredible, and perhaps that's why the predictions for Irma were not mistaken.

Earthquakes, it should be said, have also played a part in the history of Caibarién, this being one of the more seismically active parts of Cuba.

MN:
Our region, Caibarién and Remedios, has a natural peculiarity. It is considered to be the country's second most important seismic zone after Oriente, due to a combination of natural conditions. For example, the deep Las Villas Faultline, which connects with the Trocha fault. The Caibarién fault lies close to our locality. And as a result of this, there is a series of morpho-alignments of weak tectonic alignments along the whole insular platform towards the keys. When the earth shakes in Oriente, all these plates and microplates start to readjust. And as an echo, you might say, there are earthquakes that are generally of Category 2, 3 or 3.5. Often imperceptible, but at certain moments they have had a big impact.

The earthquake of 15th August 1939 is famous. It was felt in Caibarién and Remedios, but it was also felt in Cienfuegos, in Placetas, in Cabaiguán, in places that were distant from the locality. And it caused fear in the population. When it happened, around midnight, the people went out to the street in their pyjamas, and others in their underwear, because of the terror that the earthquake provoked, along with the associated noise.

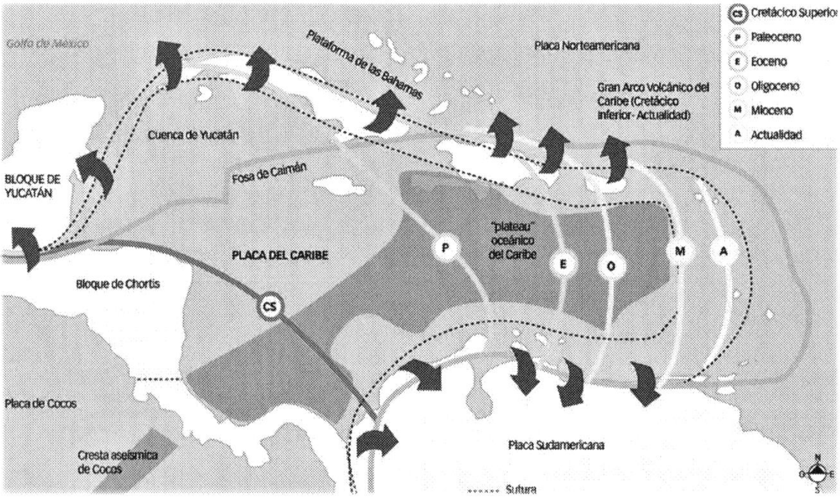

Seismic dangers in the Caribbean
Source: Servicio Sismológico Nacional, Mexico

When CENAIS (the National Centre for Seismological Research) was established in Santiago de Cuba three years ago, a seismological station was installed in the meteorological station where I work, in order to monitor the seismic movements. In my personal experience (and I have lived through a few), the seismic events that are perceptible result in shaking cups or glasses, or one feels the earth moving – which would be a quake of magnitude 3, or a little bit more. This happens every six or seven years. Although those that aren't perceptible are more frequent. But we have never been affected by a tidal wave. There has never been a tsunami.

Whether a tremor or a hurricane, or any other such natural event, the Cuban state actively seeks not only to provide adequate warning – and for this to be conveyed to the population as a whole – but also guarantee coordinated responses from the various national, regional and local organisations.

AC:
Evidently, thanks to the close collaboration, we have always been very successful, and the population has complete confidence in all the warnings that we transmit. And something else needs to be mentioned, there is only one voice. The voice of our Institute of Meteorology. All the television channels broadcast our position. There is no place for external rumours. There is only one idea, which is that of the Institute of Meteorology, the perspective that we provide, and that is transmitted by the media and is managed by national Civil Defence, which is in constant coordination with our forecast centre.

But however much preparation there has been, nothing can be done to prevent damage from occurring; and however much the state might seek to keep the population thoroughly informed, when the hurricane arrives all depends upon local responses – both collective and individual.

AC:
The telephone system collapses. The utility poles fall, the trees fall on houses and everything that comes between them. And so, it becomes a disaster situation.

AC:
All that can be humanly done is to try to minimise the impact of disasters, above all the number of deaths, which in the case of hurricanes in Cuba have been minimal thanks to the joint actions taken by our national Civil Defence, and our Meteorological Forecast Centre, with our technicians specialised in tropical cyclone warnings and early alarm systems – early warning for those organisations that are involved in managing this kind of emergency. People need to have a mobile phone to hear the warnings, or somebody who can communicate them. And so there can be an atmosphere of uncertainty, because the latest updates cannot be heard.

LER:
It is inevitable that there are material losses. It depends upon a great deal of factors, which sometimes from a human point of view cannot be controlled. But the preservation of life remains the priority, above all in those small communities that, if we look 60 or 70 years ago, were completely forgotten about, because no meteorological information reached them. Today, though, there is an interconnection between different lines of communication, and if there is anywhere that the message doesn't reach then you can be sure that somebody will personally travel there in order to take the information, and to evacuate if necessary those people living in danger zones.

AF:
For example, in Batabanó – which is one of the zones of greatest impact when hurricanes enter from the South – there have been moments in which people have been evacuated with all their belongings. But this is very costly to do. You can't go doing it every year. Here there was a very humane policy – but the country couldn't afford to maintain it – which was to give people replacements for all that they had lost. A mattress, a television, a fridge. They lost it, and the state replaced it. That is something that could be done once every ten years, every fifteen years. But not every year that a hurricane passes.

Since there is a need for individuals to be able to take responsibility for themselves and their community when circumstances require, Cuba pays a lot of attention to educating the population about such natural events, and how to deal with them.

MI:
The fundamental focus should be on children and young people. Of course, when you focus on the child or youth, indirectly you are focusing on the family, because the children go to ask their father or mother, or whoever, and so we can succeed in incorporating ideas into the family through them.

AC:
When we are children, they teach us about hurricanes in geography classes. This education of the population is included in the curricula for secondary schools and sixth forms. In medical degrees, courses on disaster medicine are given.

In the geography books, the danger of hurricanes is spoken about. The triple threat that hurricanes have: hurricane-strength winds, intense rain, and the effects of the sea, which can be multiple. There might be storm surges, waves generated by winds, and hurricane-generated waves. Above all, when the hurricane touches land, on the right-hand side of the trajectory of its centre the sea is capable of penetrating the coast, sometimes tens of kilometres inland. And the storms – one sees the tornados that can accompany a hurricane.

I believe that education in Cuba is a complete success. It means the population is well prepared. Of course, we always worry that there are zones that are hit more by hurricanes, and zones hit less by hurricanes. When there are zones hit more by hurricanes, the people are more accustomed to the phenomenon as it is very common. And in the zones where hurricanes pass only infrequently, people are more relaxed, because they say that it has been a hundred years since a Category 5 hurricane has passed, and until you see one in reality, you don't know what the danger is like when you are really caught up inside the body of a hurricane.

Education, of course, should not be seen as something that stops at the schools, but which continues throughout life, and into the community. In Cuba, programmes exist with this in mind. From the national down to the local level, exercises are regularly carried out to ensure general preparedness, not just of those whose direct responsibility it will be to deal with the effects of a potential disaster, but the public as well.

Participants in the Meteoro exercise (2019)
Source: Radio Reloj

MN:
Every year in May, before the start of the hurricane season, a preparatory exercise is carried out in Cuba, which is called Meteoro. In this the population and those who direct the defensive activities are given preparation.

AC:
Every year it is focused on a different type of threat. That is, different hydrometeorological phenomena: tornados, intense rain, hurricanes or seismic phenomena, as there are some regions in Cuba that experience these. There is publicity. Leaflets are made.

Nevertheless, there is a perception amongst those most directly involved in the field that still more could be done to prepare the general population, to make them more aware of the dangers, as well as the measures they can take to help mitigate the impact of hurricanes and the like. This is perhaps becoming all the more necessary as climatic changes seem to be intensifying such events.

AC:
I believe we still have a lot to do. At least in terms of publicity, to advise the population as to what can happen with intense hurricanes, the different categories of hurricane, the different phenomena that can be associated with an intense hurricane. Evidently in the educational curricula there is a need, from when children are in primary school, to spread this kind of culture towards an understanding of a phenomenon with which we have to live.

The *Fundación Antonio Nuñez Jiménez de la Naturaleza y el Hombre* – the Cuban partners of the *Living Between Hurricanes* documentary production, and associated research network – have been involved in the raising of public awareness.

LN:
We realised that communication was very important at every level of direction and participation in the country, in all sectors. All the work of Civil Defence is so efficient, preparing for the cyclonic periods, planning for evacuations, assistance to the evacuees, attention to how to get the electric grid working again. But there isn't the same level of efficiency amongst the other organisations of the central state administration – the state being the principal economic actor in Cuba – nor in the other sectors of society.

We have carried out many audiovisual campaigns, on the television – which fortunately in Cuba is public. Publicity spots for public welfare campaigns, which we don't have to pay for. It is a big advantage for social communication.

I believe that this is like a spiral, with every hurricane leaving a lesson, which combined with the state's plan for confronting climate change, results in a widespread divulgation, in whatever sector or whatever community, of the precepts that help to understand a little about how to prepare between hurricanes.

LER:
Fundamentally they are helping to raise public consciousness, in the sense of bolstering what has been done over the last fifty years through all the national state programmes.

LER:
The territorial governments have never stopped insisting on the necessity to protect themselves against hurricanes, nor have they scrimped on resources to evacuate the population. That is a reality, it is a truth. And I can say that having carried out a historical analysis of the victims caused by hurricanes throughout the meteorological history of Cuba, most of the people who have died in the last forty years have done so due to the carelessness of those who have not followed the instructions for protecting themselves. But the state carries out large-scale programmes for educating people on how to protect themselves from hurricanes. And does not scrimp on the resources for moving threatened populations, evacuating them, taking them to places where they can stay until the danger has passed.

With rising sea levels, coastal populations in Cuba, as elsewhere around the world, are likely to face greater threats; and as a result, it will be increasingly necessary to take long-term measures to cope with this reality.

MI:
Nature, or the planet, functions, it has its mechanism. Sometimes we think that an event only occurs once. I always say that if an event has occurred once, then it will be repeated. One has to be prepared for it.

LER:
In fact, there are places in Cuba where it has been necessary to persuade the people who live there that there are particular settlements, especially on the coasts, that are dangerous, and that it is recommendable to move the population from their place of origin. It's normal for people to cling to the place where they have always lived, and to want to conserve where perhaps they were born, have lived their first years, and so they have some resistance to change.

MI:
In the case of Hurricane Irma, we drew the following conclusions. Whoever didn't take the touble of building on piles (*pilotes*), on low ground that is normally flooded, again had their houses flooded. Either build your house on piles, or don't continue building there. If you have a house with a flat roof, then the roof fell on your head, because it wasn't designed to withstand so much rain. But those who built sloping roofs didn't have a problem.

There is a community in the north of Camagüey where the houses are built on piles, but the modern houses are on the ground. I have photographed houses in Mayarí that are built on piles, old wooden houses. I don't know how old, but still there. Then others have built on the ground, where all the mud comes in, and the house is destroyed by the first hurricane.

Here in Havana itself, the old houses in the low part of Vedado were tall. Today we make houses with tunnels underneath, with basements. But I keep saying that you shouldn't put the life of a building, the survival of a building, its water supply, its electricity etcetera, where the first flood stops it working. But we don't learn.

LER:
In reality, I believe that the policy consists in continuing to explain, continuing to keep people informed, offering them the meteorological culture and environmental information necessary for them to understand that, for particular reasons, it will be necessary in many cases to transform the natural environment. Transformations in the places where they live, because the climate is not exactly the same as it was some years ago. The meteorological panorama that we might have had a hundred years ago, is changed now, largely due to the changes caused by the economic transformations.

But there is an unarguable fact, which is that the climate is variable, and changes, and this also influences not only the intensity of hurricanes, but also the form in which, from the point of view of geographic space, they impact on the population, and on agriculture, and on material resources in general.

So I believe that it is just necessary to give continuity, and to perfect the form and methods and style with which the campaigns for educating the public have been carried out. But I can assure you that in the last fifty years, the programmes foreseen by the state for trying to avoid at all costs the loss of life, in first place, and the preservation of natural resources, in second place, material resources, in third place, have been in place throughout these years.

Certainly, hurricanes can have a devastating effect, and for this reason it is so important to be prepared for living with the reality of their likelihood. However, sight should not be lost of the truth that hurricanes are simply a natural phenomenon, and while their high winds and sea surges may bring immediate damage, in the long-term the rain that they dump in their passing plays a crucial role in the maintenance of a healthy ecosystem in the regions where they are prevalent.

AC:
You have to see this as a part of nature. The earth didn't give these things in order to kill, nor to cause damage. Hurricanes produce beneficial rains. Thanks to Hurricane Irma, after three years of drought Cuba recovered the deficit in the subsoil. The subterranean waters in the central region of Cuba afterwards were around 137 percent over the average rainfall needed in the month of September.

The rain from a hurricane goes into the water catchment areas, into deep aquifers. It fills the reservoirs. It helps agriculture. It cleans the river basins. In places where there is 'red tide' (*marea roja*) caused by microorganisms, it breaks this down, cleaning the river basins. It reconstructs the sandy-bar islands. Afterwards wildlife flourishes.

FF:
In reality, extreme climatic events always happen. There's always an extreme climatic event. But hurricanes have much more dramatic repercussions. A hurricane goes by at a particular moment, just like a tornado. But probably in Cuba drought causes more problems than hurricanes. Strong rains cause more problems than hurricanes.

Antonio Núñez Jiménez (revolutionary leader and a great pioneer in exploring and, importantly, understanding the environment of Cuba and Latin America, whose memory continues to inspire) often pointed out the truth that hurricanes formed a necessary part of the Caribbean's water cycle. The Cuban Foundation that carries his name continues to work to develop an awareness of this, and other ways in which humans need to find a harmony with the natural processes that surround them.

RF:
I recall that Núñez Jiménez said that they were like a factory of water, and that Cuba needed hurricanes in order to produce water.

Antonio Núñez Jiménez

Hurricanes might capture the international headlines, but it is lack of water that has a far more damaging impact, in the long term, on the life of an island such as Cuba.

FF:
We are now passing through a critical event. The rains should have started in May. But it practically didn't rain in May. It only rained twice, but that doesn't mean anything. I was reading an article that says that at least 25 percent of the country has not had sufficient rain in May, June and July. These are the months when it usually begins to rain. So although it rained a couple of times, that made no difference to the water table. In fact it can be more problematic, because when it rains one day and the next there is a lot of sun, then it affects the crops, particularly when these are leafy vegetables.

Despite all the efforts we have made, we are now in a water crisis, because the wells have not recovered. We hoped that at the start of May they would begin to recover, but over two months have gone by, and the wells have still not begun to refill.

AC:
Hurricanes, from one point of view, are beneficial. If there hasn't been a hurricane for a long period, there isn't rain. For example, the agriculture of Baja California peninsula and the north east of Mexican Sonora depends on tropical cyclones for 75 percent of its rain. When there aren't any cyclones, they have a drought. So we need to see the positive side of hurricanes.

Although there is a tendency to portray hurricanes, and other such extreme events, as being disasters, in truth they are nothing more than natural occurrences. It is our human responses to these that define whether they will be a disaster or not. They are simply what they are. It is how well we cope with them, and succeed in living with them, that determines whether or not they result in catastrophe.

MI:
Disasters come from human presence. That is to say, nature has a volcano, and that isn't a disaster, it's a volcano. An earthquake is simply the Earth's crust moving. That isn't a disaster, it is the movement of the Earth's crust. Whether it's big, small or middling, it is thanks to this that the Earth was formed. That the solar system was formed. It is a way in which the universe exists. There are droughts, fine, that is also a natural process. If it rains a lot and there are floods, well that as well. That is to say, all the events that occur in nature are absolutely normal. And we cannot control that.

AC:
We could say that a hurricane in a region produces a disaster if humans are there. If humans don't exist, then there isn't any disaster. The hurricane is something created by nature, because it performs a function. One of its principal functions is to lower the surface temperature of the sea. The swell produced by a hurricane produces a phenomenon that is the upsurge of cooler water from the ocean bed. This rises up with the swell, and the sea temperature is freshened and it leaves a cold print. And that is part of the equilibrium that there is between the parts that make up Mother Nature.

4 Rise and Fall of a Port

Caibarién is the exit port for Remedios. That is the key.

Hernán Venegas

Although the town of Caibarién itself was not founded until the nineteenth century, the area has been populated from long before the arrival of the Spanish in the sixteenth century.

AM:
In 1981 we found in the large cave at Guajabana, an archaeological funeral site, with manufacturing activities using shaped stones. And it seems that it was a refuge, because a wide range of dietary waste was also found. After that, we began to explore the whole municipality, and at the moment we have found more than 61 sites where there is clear aboriginal evidence – whether of long-term settlement, or the result of movement around the island.

In Caibarién we have found remains of the oldest aboriginal culture in Cuba – the famous protoarchaic culture, seen in the shaping of stone. We have pottery. We have all these manifestations of aboriginal culture in the municipality. Thousands and thousands of pieces.

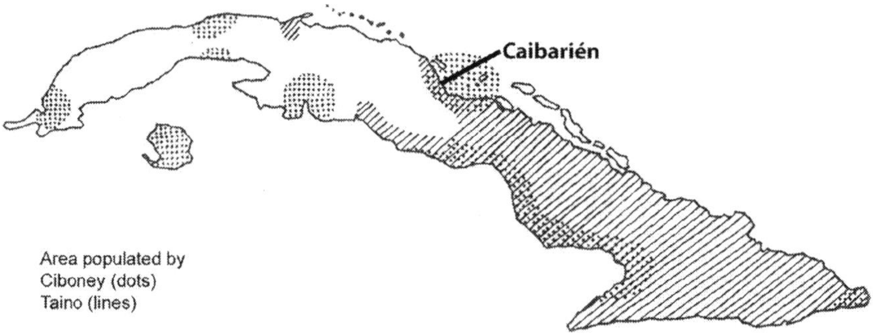

Precolumbian settlement in Cuba
Map: Dr Antonio Rafael de la Coya

AM:
The large cave that we found, is the only fluvial cave that we have in Caibarién – that is, that was formed by the action of a river. It is 80 metres above sea level at present, or rather above the base of the hill, and was formed when the plane was at that altitude. Then the famous River Guaní (which is now completely polluted) formed that cave. And it has a very important archaeological site inside. Even with pictographs. Pictographs have been found there, carved into the rock inside the cave.

Maps plotting the location of precolumbian settlements in Cuba show how important the Caibarién area, and its neighbouring islands, were, with a coincidence there of both Ciboney and Taino peoples. In 1513, the Spaniard Pánfilo de Narváez explored the district, and found on the cove an Indian village named 'Caybarien'. Nearby, on Cayo Conuco, there was another settlement, 'Carahato'.

Over the following two centuries, the area became used as a livestock estate by the Spanish settlers, dependent upon San Juan de los Remedios, the principal town in the region, just five miles inland from the present location of Caibarién. In 1703, numerous indigenous people were still to be found inhabiting the cove and neighbouring keys.

HV:
Remedios was one of the first towns to be established. Normally we speak of there being seven original settlements, and Remedios was the eighth. But it is not entirely clear when it was founded. It was probably in the 1520s. What is important is that from there the agricultural development of the region began – just as with the others, like Villa Clara, Trinidad, Sancti Spíritus. Well, Villa Clara was some time later. But it was in that order: Trinidad, Sancti Spíritus and Remedios.

OZ:
Remedios was quite autonomous, from the very circumstances under which it appeared. The town was freely founded, not by a governor. It was called the eighth town of the conquest, because it was founded by one of the chiefs of the army with whom Diego Velázquez arrived in Cuba. A man who also had connections to the Castilian aristocracy, who acquired quite an influential position and founded this town on his land. Which is why this is a freely founded town, because it wasn't officially established.

Cueva Grande de Guajabana, Caibarién
Photo: Eliecer Turó González

OZ:
Basically they lived from skins, and meats, that they exported to the Spanish colonies of Florida, and kept for their own consumption. It is probable that cacao was introduced as a product for local consumption, which is how tobacco must also have come to be sown, and sugarcane – although there wasn't any mill to grind it. And those were the characteristics of the Remedian economy in the seventeenth century.

So Remedios was a little on the margins, as were nearly all Cuban towns, with the exception of Havana – which was connected to the mercantile circuits since the creation of the fleet system in the mid-sixteenth century. The others had to connect to Havana in order to export, because that was the only port that had an international connection.

Throughout the seventeenth and into the eighteenth century, the inhabitants of the area had to deal with the ever-present risk of attacks from the sea.

PG:
Initially this zone, in its foundational times, was often attacked by the pirates and corsairs. The Bay of Carahatas was completely infested by pirates that assaulted Remedios. In fact the foundation of Caibarién was partly a result of this need to avoid the assaults. Fleeing from these invasions by corsairs and pirates who lived in the Bay of Carahatas, they took over Caibarién, which was more open, but shallower, where the ships didn't enter because they would be grounded.

For example, in 1650, the cove was used by pirates as a base to launch an assault on San Juan de los Remedios. This was one of the motivations behind the move further inland by a number of locals in the 1680s, immortalised in Fernando Ortiz's book *History of a Cuban Struggle Against the Demons* (*Historia de una pelea cubana contra los demonios*) and Tomás Guiterrez Alea's film adaptation – resulting in the foundation of Santa Clara. Those who remained continued to have to deal with occasional incursions, not just from pirates but also rival nations – in particular the English and Dutch.

OZ:
In reality Remedios, like Bayamo and to a certain extent Trinidad, by the seventeenth century was living from contraband. There was a complicated relationship with the pirates who were also smugglers.

There were, of course, defensive reasons that made it advisable to move the population inland, so as to be less exposed to attacks by pirates, because the relationship with the pirates was complicated. Sometimes they traded, smuggled, but at times they came and assaulted, if they didn't agree with the trade deal. There is the famous case, foundational for Cuban literature [Silvestre de Balboa's epic poem of 1608, *Espejo de paciencia*], in which this situation is experienced in Bayamo. That is, the pirates arrived, trade, and suddenly there is a disagreement. They kidnap the bishop, and there is a fight. They succeed in killing the chief of the pirates, and finish off that expedition.

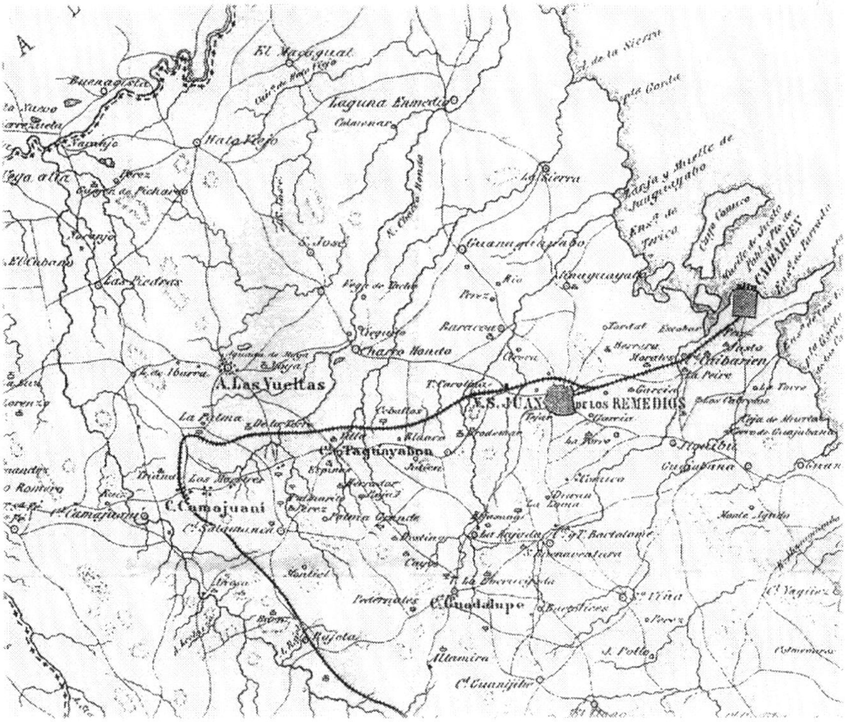

19th-century map, showing relationship of Caibarién to Remedios

War between the European powers provided a constant background throughout the eighteenth century, and into the nineteenth. Alarms were often sounded along the coast out of fear of the English or French launching attacks. Although there was a port here, Tesico (where cannons were installed in 1811 to try to deter incursions), such fears slowed down the growth of the local population.

In addition to smuggling, the main contribution of Caibarién to the Remedios economy during the early eighteenth century was from livestock. However, the region as a whole was still heavily forested at this time – and wood was an important export.

> *RF:*
> It was a zone that had a lot of forests, with precious woods. These precious woods were famous, with those used in the Escorial [royal palace in Spain], for example, coming from these territories.

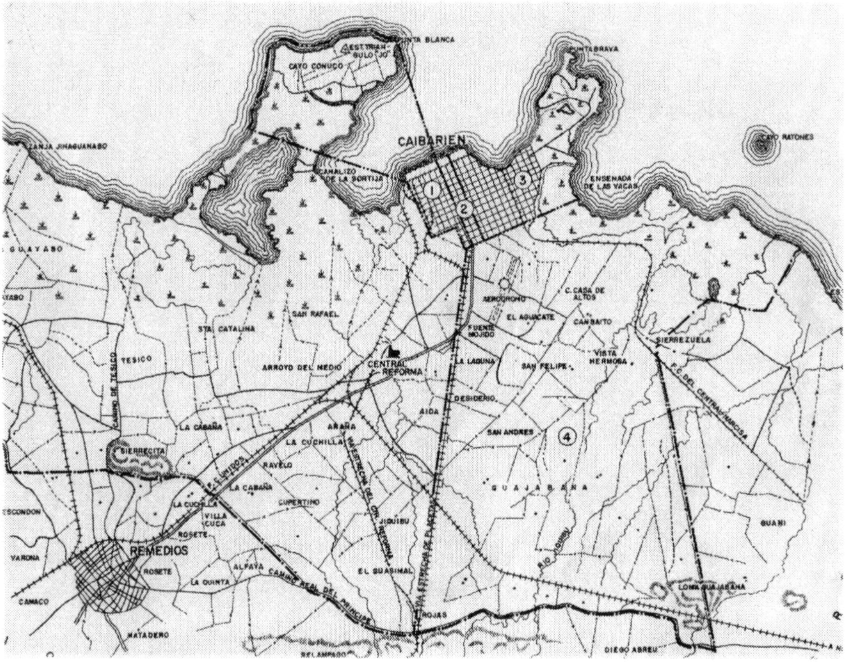

Map of Caibarién and environs (1953)

Source: *Atlas Censo 1953*, Oficina Nacional de los Censos Demográfico y Electoral, Cuba

Afterwards for naval construction, it was considered to be one of the richest forest zones, much of which was used in the Arsenal of Havana in the second half of the eighteenth century. And there was a lot of trade in wood, above all with Havana.

Slowly, a more diverse economy developed. There were some small sugar mills, such as that of 'Guajabana', also known as 'Xiquibú'; and smallholdings, with varied crops such as pineapple and cacao, alongside sugarcane.

OZ:
Although Remedios gradually develops, by the end of the eighteenth century it was still a relatively poor economy.

The local chronicles, compiled by José Martínez-Fortún, give a vivid description of what the area of Caibarién was like at the start of the nineteenth century:

> Up until this date, there were people living in the vicinity, distributed between the coves, estates, sugar mills, farms and smallholdings. Some were dedicated to fishing, others to sea-related work and the rest to agriculture. Almost all lived in palm leaf-roofed houses, and the landowners in more comfortable houses in the town of San Juan de los Remedios. The roads continued to be obstructed so as to make it harder for those enemies invading from the sea.
>
> The country folk would get up early and drink chocolate or coffee; at eight they fed on pork, fried plantain and roasted corn chocolate; at twelve they ate stew and rice, slept the siesta, returned to work, and in the afternoon had chocolate and bread, and they went to bed very early.
>
> For amusement, they would visit 'The Town' (Remedios), where the authorities were, and they contributed to the large parties on the days of Holy Week, San Juan (the patron saint), San Pedro, Santa Ana and on the visits by the bishops, higher authorities and those favourably related to the royal family in Madrid.
>
> The quiet life of the neighbourhood was interrupted from time to time by natural occurrences (storms, droughts, illnesses, etc.), by the provocations caused by the wars sustained by the dominant nations (English, French, Dutch), and by the struggles that frequently took place between the landowners, or between them and their tenants.
>
> From 1766, the black slave population began to increase.

Although there had always been people living around what is now Caibarién, it was not until the nineteenth century that it was formally founded. In 1796, the cove of Tesico was officially authorised, by royal order, as a minor port. In 1813, requests were made to the national authorities to allow for better fortification of Tesico and Caibarién; while in 1817, official negotiations were underway to transfer the port itself to Caibarién. Gradually more settlers arrived in the area, and in 1822 a local landowner, Narciso de Justa, granted lands for the building of a town, which was finally founded on 26th October 1832. Although initially given the name 'Colonia de Vives', by 1837 the original name of Caibarién had been restored.

AAG:
In the nineteenth century, when Caibarién was founded, it was still under Spanish aegis, and with Spanish sentiment. Caibarién is the daughter of San Juan de los Remedios, and it was founded by the inhabitants of Remedios. They moved, and founded what was known as the 'Colonia de Vives'. Around 1826, permission was given to establish the new town, as a politico-administrative adjunct to Remedios.

Caibarién slowly grew. In 1836, 103 people lived there; by 1845, there were 44 houses and 345 inhabitants; while in 1852, the population passed 800.

AAG:
Although Caibarién was founded in the Spanish colonial period, it was at a time when North American capital was strongly increasing. Caibarién developed in a commercial way, with a commercial bourgeoisie. While the bourgeoisie of Remedios was somewhat impregnated with the old traditions of an old-fashioned aristocracy, and was very linked to the land and production, Caibarién was linked to the sea and exports. Caibarién had a protestant maritime, bourgeois mercantile tradition. Unlike Remedios, which had a landowning bourgeois tradition, connected to the interests of the monarchy – very traditionalist and reactionary. They are two towns that are very close to one another – seven kilometres. But the idiosyncrasy of each is radically different: despite the historic ties.

While sugar had played only a minor role in the local economy hitherto, as the nineteenth century progressed and the sugar frontier expanded into the region, it became increasingly important to the local economy – as was also happening elsewhere in Cuba.

> *HV:*
> Remedios fits into a typical pattern, common to this part of the island – the Habana-Matanzas plain, which was the principal producer of sugar and its derivatives. The central regions, above all Trinidad to the south and Remedios in the north, are incorporated in this regard. It is a process typical of slave-based sugar plantation, which is oriented towards the world capitalist market. This in effect contributed to the removal of the ancient divisions into *haciendas comuneras*, for example. These are removed because the land very quickly acquired value.

The *hacienda* of Caybarién had itself been dismantled in 1820, making

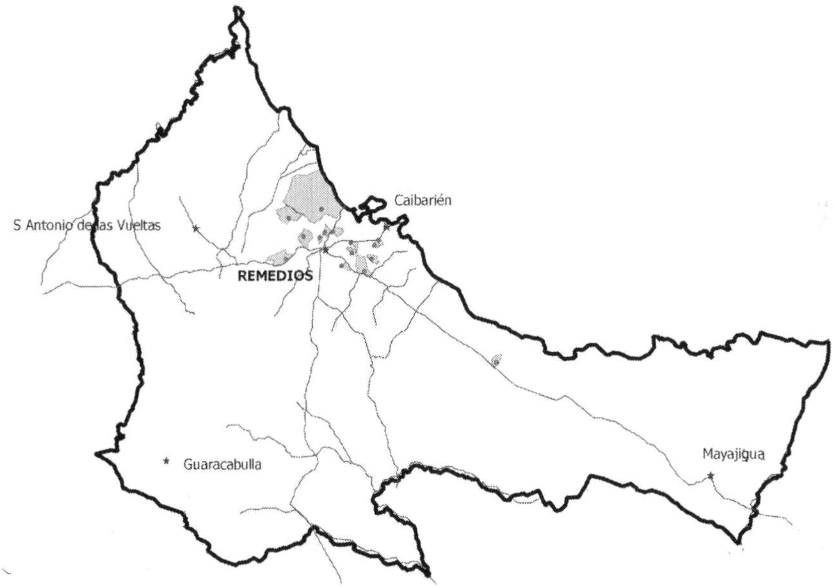

Sugar cultivation, Remedios area (1838)
Map constructed by Author from own research

way for the development of the town, as well as a more commercially-oriented agriculture in place of the previously dominant cattle ranching.

HV:
Later, when slave-based sugar manufacture began to be developed, Remedios was important in the north part of Las Villas [now Villa Clara], the centre of Cuba. It starts to abandon its initial stockbreeding character in favour of sugar.

OZ:
What happened is that the principal landowners have at least sufficient socioeconomic force, on their own initiative, to try to incorporate the sugar expansion. Of course, Trinidad to the south does this with much greater success, and much earlier. Trinidad, in the first two or three decades of the nineteenth century, is, after Havana, the principal sugar-producing zone on the island. Remedios isn't. It remains quite left behind, and in fact sugar production doesn't reach any commercial importance there until the 1830s, start of the 1840s, by which time there was some exporting.

HV:
These were lands that had never had sugarcane grown on them. They were very fertile, very productive. This changed later, towards the end of the nineteenth century, because the soils became exhausted. They become land that does not have the necessary nutrients to continue with large-scale sugar production. But in the nineteenth century Remedios became adapted to these development patterns. It had good soils, and at least until the start of the twentieth century this gave good results.

One sugar mill close to Caibarién was the Dolores, the remains of whose buildings can still be seen today.

NQ:
The Dolores mill was established by José María Vissinay, who ordered the construction of this building, with a workforce of slaves brought from Africa.

Dolores sugar mill, with improvised accommodation for local families (2019)
Photos: Gonzalo Vidal

NQ:

In the vicinity [of Dolores] shackles have been found, as evidence of that colonial era of slavery. Gold coins have also been found. These have been lost over the years, while the shackles we donated to the municipal museum.

José María Vissinay, who was the first owner of this place, gave it the name of Dolores after his wife. The tower is similar to the Iznaga Tower in Sancti Spíritus. There are some people who say that this is considered to be the second Iznaga tower in the country, because it was built in the same period, with several levels – although the other one is much taller, this one has four levels.

Many slaves died. They were treated badly, and many died from illnesses. The anthropologists have been looking for a burial ground, but they haven't been able to find it. I speak to the children here sometimes. This is a humble community, where they have to make their latrines and so on, for which they have to dig in the ground. And I tell them to let me know if they find any human bones. But they haven't found any.

Ingenio Manaca-Iznaga, Trinidad (1857)
Lithography by Eduardo Laplante

A *babalao* once came here to visit, and he said: 'I can't be on this land, because there are dead bodies buried here.' He hadn't studied the area, nor worked on it, so it drew my attention that he should say that. So we have been searching for the slave cemetery that Dolores has. We have even found aboriginal spoons, dating from an earlier period. When the rivers rise, they leave behind aboriginal spoons, which we have also given to the municipal museum.

From starting the nineteenth century as a marginal zone, as the sugar frontier took a hold the Remedios region as a whole began to increase in importance.

OZ:
I think that basically they took advantage of the moment. The big expansion in slave-plantation sugar takes place between 1830 and 1860, the second third of the nineteenth century, and Remedios to a certain extent is incorporated into this expansive movement.

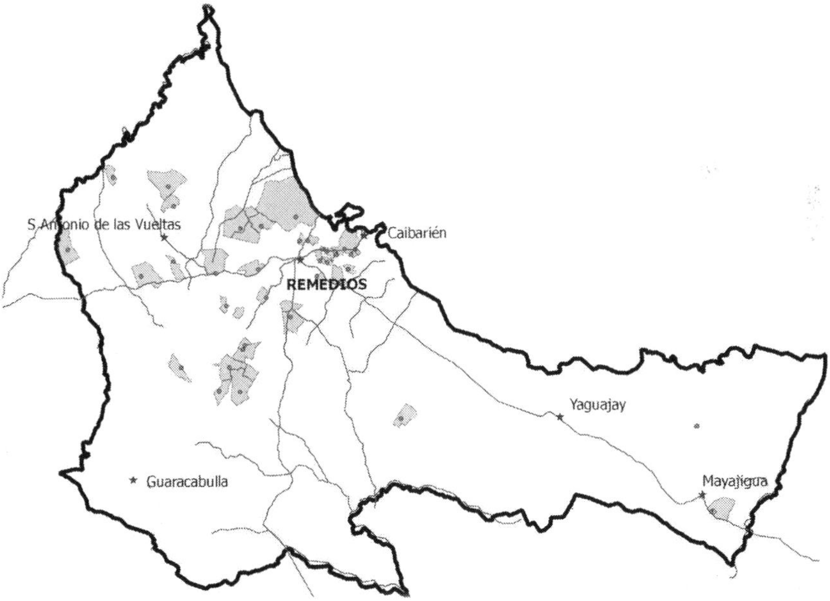

Sugar cultivation, Remedios area (1848)
Map constructed by Author from own research

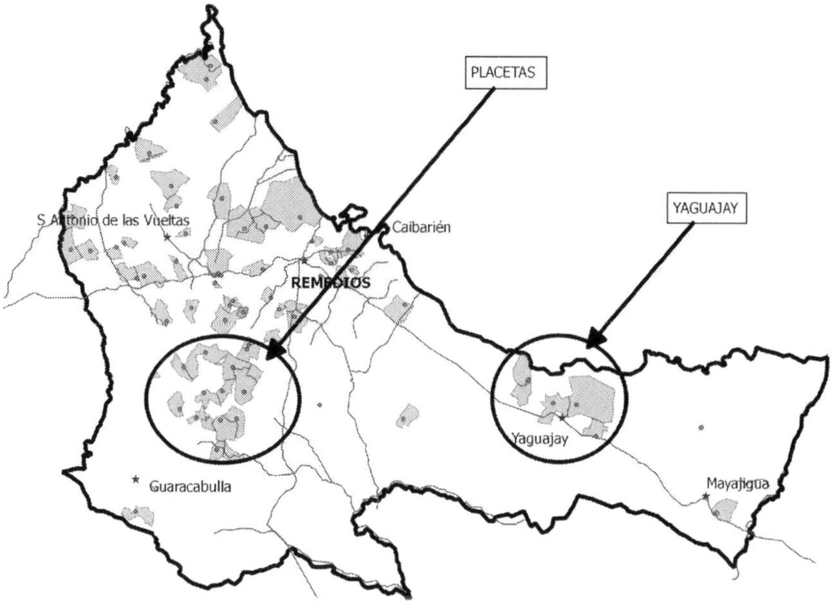

Sugar cultivation, Remedios area, 1858
Map constructed by Author from own research

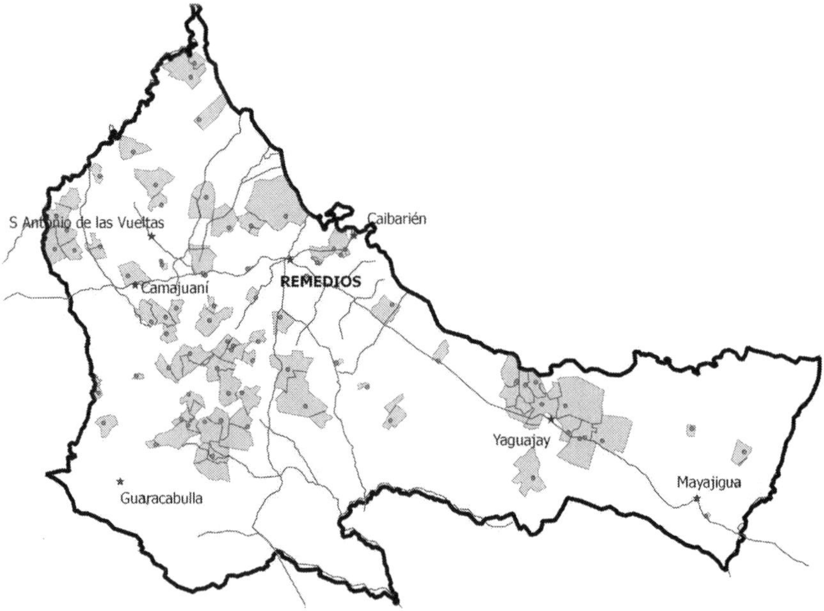

Sugar cultivation, Remedios area, 1868
Map constructed by Author from own research

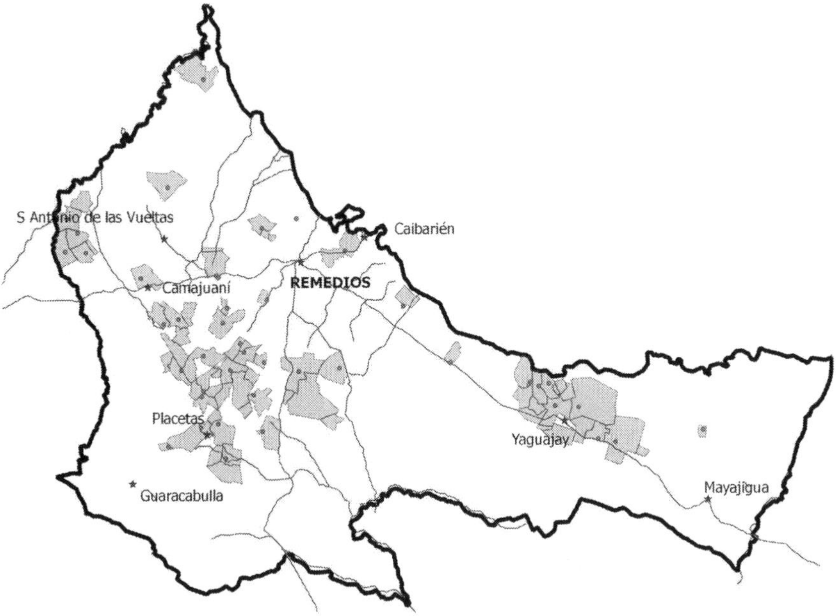

Sugar cultivation, Remedios area, 1878
Map constructed by Author from own research

OZ:
Remedios became incorporated into the sugar frontier through its own efforts, to a certain extent autonomously. Probably because they were already able to more clearly identify commercial partners, and take advantage of the resources that were already present in order to import the technology. And I think that the presence there of those first North Americans, who established some mills in the area, is important.

Although Caibarién was situated on the coast, it was by no means obvious that it would acquire the commercial importance it had achieved by the twentieth century. After all, its bay was shallow and not suitable for deep-hulled ships, while the roads inland were notoriously poor. However, this changed as railways came early to Cuba.

Sugar railroad, Victoria plantation, Yaguajay (1901)
Photo courtesy of Reinaldo Funes Monzote

OZ:
The most important figures that I have seen in this economic push of the 1830s and 40s, ere those who were the promotors of the small rail line between Remedios and Caibarién. These were [Colonel Manuel J. de] Rojas – who had been mayor, and was probably the richest man in the town – and his nephew, Estratón Bausa. These two are the ones who developed the railway and, evidently, were the people with most economic power. There were probably North American investors or landowners who had established themselves in the area, and set up mills. But evidently, economic power was in creole hands in the town.

Caibarién is practically the offspring of the railway initiative, because they had been exporting from a landing point at a place called Tesico. This was a cove perhaps closer to Remedios, but not so well-suited to function as a port.

AAG:
It was much easier to finance the railways from the plantation zone to the north coast, where there were towns like Cárdenas, like Matanzas, like Sagua la Grande, Caibarién, where there was production and export.

In 1845, the first measures were taken to establish a rail line between Caibarién and Remedios, with construction beginning in 1850. With just five miles separating the two towns, it was quickly finished, and train services began in 1851.

OZ:
The first small railway line, between Remedios and Caibarién, is from the 1840s. It was built before even the Sagua railway. Of course, the growth of the Remedios-Caibarién network happens later.

Whether or not the construction of the railway itself stimulated sugar production in the Remedios area is perhaps something of a chicken-and-egg question. But clearly the local sugar industry was booming. From having 37 sugar mills in 1846, by 1851 this had grown to 51, while the value of exports through Caibarién quadrupled.

The rail network eventually connected much of the region, linking Caibarién inland to Santa Clara (and the rail routes running down the spine of the island), and along the coast to the sugar plantation zones of Yaguajay,

Train station, Caibarién (1910)
Postcard, courtesy of Pedro Manuel González Reinoso

Map of train routes, Cuba (present day)
Source: Maps Cuba

Morón and Nuevitas. Many of the lines that today continue to make up the Cuban rail system were intially built specifically to service the sugar industry – as, for example, the narrow-gauge route that directly connected the large Zaza sugar factory near Placetas to the port, of which other mills in the area took advantage.

> *HV:*
> As the nineteenth century advanced, when there weren't good ports, the railways provided a solution to the problem. Moving production. Not just production for export, but the influx of all kinds of machinery, or whatever. Brought from the United States, England, and France.
>
> *OZ:*
> As the sugar frontier expanded into the interior of the island, the further away from the coast it got the more the costs of transport increased, and the railways served to reduce these transport costs. So the movement of sugar plantations into the interior is very connected to the railways.

It was these connections that gave to Caibarién its increasing economic importance.

AAG:
The development of Caibarién coincided with the sugar boom. But not so much because of the plantations. Caibarién only had one sugar factory, the Reforma. The principal sugar-related activity was not production, but its export and the shipping trade. Because it was much easier to import into the United States directly from the north coast of Cuba, than to go from the important southern ports, such as Cienfuegos or Santiago de Cuba. The north coast was easier.

It was because of this that a mercantile bourgeoisie developed, with a lot of influence from the United States. Protestantism arrived in force, while Remedios remained traditionalist, catholic and rural, with elements of a rural aristocracy. Caibarién was always bourgeois and protestant.

Docks in Caibarién (early 20th century)
Photo courtesy of Pedro Manuel González Reinoso

HV:
Every region has its exit ports: for example, in the case of Trinidad, it's the port of Casilda, and other secondary embarkations. Cienfuegos has an excellent bay, which is why sugar slave-plantation agriculture develops there from 1819.

A port system was established, although the port of Caibarién did not have good conditions. It wasn't a deep port, like that of Jagua or Matanzas; nor wide, like that of Antilla in the Nipe region, or Guantánamo Bay and the bay of Santiago. It had marshy land, often flooded. Buenavista Bay was not a deep bay. On the contrary. It is full of sediments and sand banks. The majority of the keys that are facing Caibarién are coral keys, or biogenic keys, made out of coral or mangroves. Apart from a few that are rocky, like Cayo Conuco. So, the port wasn't very good. It was a muddy port. A port that had to be drained from time to time.

Transport barges, Caibarién (early 20th century)
Photo courtesy of Pedro Manuel González Reinoso

> *PG:*
> There was a submarine corridor of a few metres. Not much, but it was something that took a long time to establish, and which periodically had to be cleaned because the mud (these are muddy bays) was deposited, and came to fill up the whole channel. This was in the nineteenth century.

Despite the practical problems of using Caibarién as a port, it developed strongly. In 1842, a steam-ship service was established, linking Caibarién by water to Sagua la Grande, and beyond – to Cárdenas, Matanzas and eventually Havana itself. In 1853, the first public dock was opened; and in 1859, good quality boats begin to be fabricated in the town.

> *HV:*
> The exports were carried in barges pulled by tugs, ancient small powerful boats. And in this way exports were made, not only from Caibarién, but from the whole of the northern region of what is now Sancti Spíritus, Yaguajay – where sugar was also sown, and which was under the jurisdiction of Caibarién in that period. And there was a very strong commercial connection with the north of Ciego de Ávila.
>
> And that motivated the construction of large warehouses, considered to be the largest in Latin America in that era. Unfortunately, today they are no more than ruins.

By 1860, Caibarién had six warehouses, alongside five docks. Although initially considered a dependency of Remedios, its commercial importance led it to become progressively more autonomous as the nineteenth century progressed.

> *AAG:*
> It wasn't until the start of the 1870s that it becomes possible to talk about Cabiarién having an independent identity. After then it developed thanks to, and always deriving from, sugar.

In 1873, Caibarién was granted the title of 'Villa', and in 1878 its population had reached five-thousand inhabitants. At last, in 1879 it was allowed to

Sugar warehouse, Caibarién (early 20th century)
Photo courtesy of Pedro Manuel González Reinoso

establish its own town council, with its first mayor, Don Hipólito Escobar Martelo.

Over this period, the importance of central Cuba for the sugar industry was steadily growing. In the Las Villas region, in which Caibarién was situated, the share in value of the island's total sugar production rose from just 6 percent in 1826, to 40 percent by the end of the century – by when it was challenging Havana and Matanzas, which hitherto had dominated the industry. However, although an increasing amount of land in the zone of Remedios was given over to cane, the area was always somewhat marginal as a producer, compared to other parts of the region.

OZ:
Remedios was always a secondary zone. Secondary even in relationship to Sagua. Sagua was a production zone that was much more important than Remedios. We could say that in the Cuban central region, in the second half of the nineteenth century, Remedios was in something like third place.

First comes Sagua and Cienfuegos, which are the two large plantation-expansion zones, they were two large productive zones. Trinidad for a time rivals Remedios, and is more important than Remedios until, say, 1840 or 1850. But it was in decline. Trinidad's production, its plantations, were very concentrated in the Valley of the Mills (*Valle de los ingenios*). A valley that had been exploited for decades, where there was a loss of fertility in the land, and a resultant decline in Trinidad. And although Trinidad of course doesn't disappear as a sugar producer, Remedios moves ahead of it. Nationally, it takes sixth or seventh place in the scale of its production.

Much of the increase in sugar production in the area of Remedios came not around Remedios itself, where the earliest local sugar mills had been situated, but on terrain that had hitherto been given over to cattle ranching, where the dismantling of the traditional *haciendas* brought an opportunity for entrepreneurs to acquire and enclose large quantities of land.

OZ:
Yaguajay and Placetas are two zones of expansion for, it could be said, the sugar capital of Remedios, because they were areas that were relatively unexploited. What happened is that, in the case of Placetas, they had to be adapted, because it was not a flat area like that of Remedios. That is, it has small elevations, hills. The industry there was well-financed, above all after the 1860s. Even some of the first centralised sugar factories – as in the case of Zaza – were founded in the Placetas area. But this was not, from an agricultural point of view, a typical sugarcane plantation zone. An undulating land. But it works above all because the landowner and merchant who founded Central Zaza, and was one of the most powerful men in the island – Julián Zulueta – extends the Remedios railway to Placetas, and integrates it with the Remedios-Caibarién line. And so it was much easier to move the sugar and export it from Caibarién.

In the case of Yaguajay, a similar thing happens to Placetas. This is a territory with mountains nearby, but with ease of appropriating land – and it is precisely for that reason, along with Placetas, that it is the other focus for expansion of Remedios, and in the process of centralisation of sugar production.

Train locomotive, Narcisa sugar mill, Yaguajay (2010)
Photo: Wilder Llanes Méndez

OZ:
In Yaguajay, the Narcisa, Victoria and Santa Catalina mills were founded, already as small centralised sugar factories, with a capacity to produce forty or fifty thousand sacks per sugar harvest.

It was in these two areas in particular that large sugar mills were developed, while most of the smaller, older, less economically viable mills closer to Remedios itself gradually fell into disuse – their lands either turned to other crops, abandoned, or farmed with cane to be processed in the increasingly rationalised centralised sugar factories.

OZ:
If we count the sugar mills that existed in the jurisdiction of Remedios in 1860, there were 35. If we go to the statistic for 1877, that is twenty years later, in Remedios we find there are only 17 mills. That is to say, in those twenty years the number of sugar mills in the Remedios area was reduced by half. In some cases they grew, and in growing they absorbed the land of the small mills.

This was the process of centralisation. But at this point it was still just incipient, it was barely beginning. It occurred above all from the second half of the 1880s and the first of the 1890s.

Caibarién of course served the export needs for much of the sugar, and other productions, of the Remedios area. Despite its natural limitations, it proved to be well-situated as a port, and sufficiently well-connected, such that it was able to service the commercial export needs of the entire region.

OZ:
The economic success of Caibarién came from not only being the exportation port for the Remedios region, and to a certain extent Yaguajay and Placetas, but also because sugars were sent to Caibarién from mills that were being established and were working around Santa Clara – which after all was daughter to Remedios.

Although the sugar industry made significant inroads into the Remedios region, and much of Caibarién's increasing wealth came from its export, unlike some other parts of the country, this area always maintained a somewhat more diverse economy.

OZ:
As a plantation zone, Remedios was quite sui generis. That is, there of course was slavery there, and throughout the period of colonial flourishing the sugar industry is sustained by slavery. But it is a zone where a small peasantry remained.

AAG:
There was wine production. There was production of sugar and its derivatives. One of the largest tanneries in Cuba. And there was also a porcine industry, a bovine industry, and some discrete agricultural production – almost always for local consumption, rather than for export.

HV:
In the case of Remedios, the other major production continues to be from cattle and its derivatives. In any case, nineteenth-century sugar manufacture needed beasts of burden.

HV:
There was also a need for animals to provide meat to sustain the slave workforce, and in general to feed the region. So there is a relationship established between one product and another.

In addition, Remedios is characterised by the production of some tobacco – and of what is known as 'Remedios leaf', which is, according to some, the second or third best leaf in Cuba, after that of Vuelta Abajo [Pinar del Río].

OZ:
Above all the area around Camajuaní developed as a tobacco zone. Although also sugarcane. The farmers who grew cane, generally didn't only grow cane. They grew crops for their own consumption, but also cultivated for the local markets. And they also had cattle, milk. Probably between a quarter and a third of the milk that was collected, came from these cane-growing farms.

Wood, which had been an important export for the region since the earliest days of Spanish settlement, continued to be traded through Caibarién – although with the increasing disappearance of the forests, this movement came to be reversed.

Wood factory and warehouse, Caibarién (early 20th century)
Photo courtesy of Pedro Manuel González Reinoso

RF:
They brought wood from the whole of this region to Caibarién to export it. Precious woods. Mahogany and cedar. And a lot of wood was imported there, which I suppose was used in the building of businesses, and the sugar factories in the area.

PG:
Hard woods were also imported from the United States. It was used to make the sleepers that supported the rail lines. These needed to be well built, with a resistant wood to withstand the weight of the wagons that came loaded with sacks of sugar. And the lines ran to the very end of the docks, from where they were laden and exported.

RF:
There is a contradiction here, in that while Cuba was destroying all its forests, the wood was leaving here through Caibarién, with its wood warehouse. All those ships carrying precious woods, while at the same time Cuba in the nineteenth century depended a great deal on the importation of all kinds of wood from the United States. If one sees the statistics, that exportation of wood declined continually. And yet Cuba was ever more dependent upon that importation of wood.

Agricultural diversity, and the growing presence of smallholder farming as the land became increasingly deforested, resulted in the influx of land-seeking immigrants.

OZ:
Above all in the area of Placetas there arrived quite an important immigration from the Canary Islands in the final three decades of the nineteenth century, for the tobacco, in those tobacco zones of Camajuaní and the area around Placetas. And also growing cane. Some cane farmers are Canary Island immigrants who arrived after 1880.

This was quite different to those parts of the country that became more solidly dependent upon the sugar plantations, and which saw the arrival of greater concentrations of African slaves and their descendants. The people of Caibarién itself, with its focus on commerce, were noticeably whiter in

Tobacco farm, Vega la Palma, Camajuaní (2013)
Photo: Wilder Llanes Méndez

hue than many other parts of the country – a racial distinction that can still be seen to this day.

> *PG:*
> Caibarién has a demographic curiosity, and that is the density of the white population compared to the minimal presence of a black population. The slaves were based more in Remedios, and they moved little because they were poor. The ones who moved were the landowners, who went to found Caibarién, Santa Clara, Sancti Spíritus. But the majority of families who settled in Caibarién were Spanish in origin – from the Canary Islands – as well as some Chinese, from Canton (we had an interesting Chinatown, which has now completely disappeared), who came to dominate trade.

The local chronicles show that the first Chinese arrived in 1847, while in 1858 some colonists from the Yucatec peninsula in Mexico also settled in the area.

PG:
But the black slaves remained on the plantations, and what Caibarién had was a port. And so to this day Caibarién has few blacks. According to the statistics I have been told, the population is some 67 percent white – not mixed.

They came from all parts of Spain. My grandfather, for example, was from a family of Asturians and Galicians. But they came from all parts of Spain, principally those zones where poverty had greatest impact, and the effect of Franquismo. Well, my grandfather came fleeing from the war, from military service. And he founded a family in Havana, and moved to Caibarién because of the prosperity that this town had.

By the end of the nineteenth century, the fortunes of Caibarién seemed to be steadily rising. The local chronicle compiled by José Martínez-Fortún summarised the situation there at the turn of the century:

> The *hacienda* had become a flourishing town with greater commercial importance than Remedios. It had more than 6,000 inhabitants, a thousand urban buildings, six schools and a budget of £25,000. It extended from the edge of the sea up to the hill. Two railways lines connecting with Placetas and several steam ships to Havana and closer ports. Its port was visited by ships from several nationalities.
>
> Its streets in bad condition made it difficult for horse-drawn carriages to circulate, but on the other hand were marvellous for the feeding of goats. Numerous warehouses gave life to the shoreline, both for the storing of sugar, and food and other products. The town's ironmongers enjoyed fame, as did the delicious ice creams and refreshing drinks sold at A. Diaz's store. The Recreation Societies frequently held dances and gatherings.
>
> The town's inhabitants were respected and had a quiet life. They ate at 10am and 5pm. At night, the men would go to the Societies and the women made or received visits from their friends. There was no luxury, and the women dressed decorously. Many romantic relations lasted for years.
>
> Rainwater was drunk, collected in large iron tanks. Lighting was obtained from *luz brilliante* [oil]. Every Sunday there was an open-air band concert in the Plaza de Armas [something that still takes place well over a century later].
>
> In 1894, the neighbourhood parties were begun. As Caibarién had so many Spanish people, parties were held on certain days like 2nd May

[commemorating the uprising in Madrid against French occupation], Santiago [patron saint of Spain, celebrated on 25th July], La Covadonga [celebrating the start of the reconquest of Spain in 718], etc. Whenever an important personage arrived, especially if this was the Captain General, then it was a 'big' day.

As Caibarién's wealth grew, this gave the opportunity for the development of other industries besides those related to sugar and exports. As well as leather goods, with the establishment in 1860 of what would become Cuba's largest tannery (and second largest in the Americas), mosaics became something of a local specialty.

AOV:
The production of mosaics in Caibarién is part of the city's industrial heritage. This mosaic production began in the nineteenth century, practically shortly after the founding of the city. And at one point it reached a peak, with five factories producing as many as two thousand tiles a day, all as a craft industry. These tiles always had 20 cm sides, and they were made with moulds made from different metals: bronze, zinc, and so on.

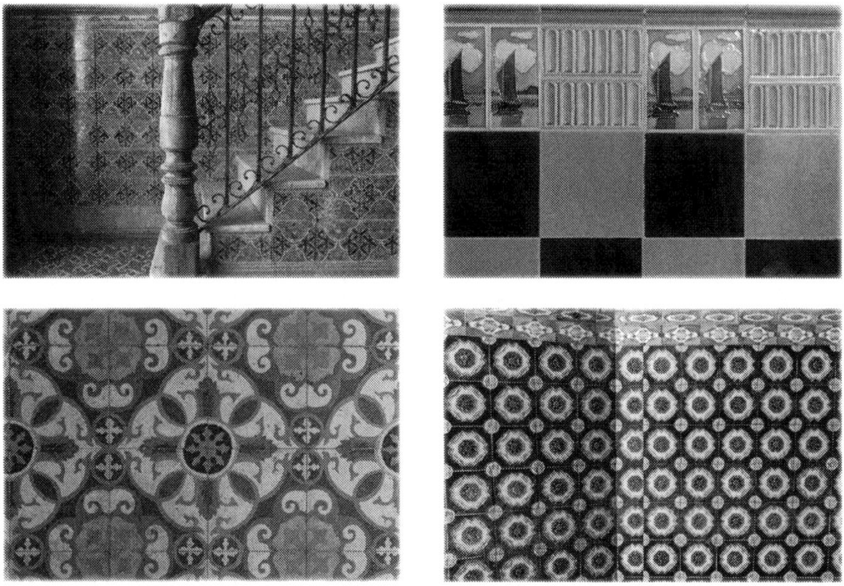

Caibarién tiles
Photos: Gonzalo Vidal

They had a catalogue of designs that the public could choose from and have ordered. And if you look around, you can see these came to make perfect tropical carpets for the decoration of floors. It was very related to the Mudejar art that flourished in Spain, with the so-called 'Catalan mosaics', for example.

And it was a tradition that lasted for a long time in the town. It was so important that at the start of the twentieth century, even though it hadn't been long established, it was already showing results. Because one factory called 'La Modernista' won the gold medal in the Great Exposition in San Francisco. This shows how consolidated this was.

These floors can be seen throughout Caibarién: there are exteriors and interiors. And they were made with powders that were imported from the United States.

But sugar continued to be behind Caibarién's increasing fortune.

HV:
Towards the end of the nineteenth century and beginning of the twentieth, Remedios took off with the process of concentration and centralisation of sugar production. This has to do with the optimisation of production. It is a phenomenon typical of advanced capitalist society, entering into the twentieth century. It meant an intensification, but an intensification that was fundamentally related to the transformation of the internal machinery of what would become central sugar factories. 'Central' because they centralised the activity of the old mills, which resulted in a much more efficient production, much more economic, in order to compete in the world market at a time of the rise of beet sugar.

While the two Cuban independence wars (1868-78 and 1895-98) brought much destruction to this region of Cuba – with a lot of military activity, both by the Spanish (with Caibarién serving as a disembarkation port) and the rebels (taking advantage of the hills) – Caibarién itself came through relatively unscathed. In the war of 1895-98, only two out of forty-nine rural properties were abandoned. Subsequently, commerce recovered quickly, giving Caibarién an increasingly cosmopolitan air, which grew as the first decades of the twentieth century progressed.

AAG:
Caibarién has changed a lot. Its architecture has changed. Caibarién was a town that was like many of those towns in South Florida, on the keys. Like those small company towns that formed around the sugar factories.

Along the streets in and out you could see porches, arcades and houses all of the same height, made out of wood, evoking that architecture that was typical of the southern United States, and which surely came from the North American influence here.

Caibarién was prosperous. In the twentieth century it had three cinemas, though by the end of the century it only had one. It had five hotels. It had international banks. There was a strong proletarian movement. The *Hermandad Ferroviaria* (Railway Brotherhood), was a very strong trade union, with a long tradition of working-class struggle. But there was also a local bourgeoisie, dedicated to exports and fishing.

The town of Remedios became unprosperous. Remedios was always subordinate to Caibarién, in economic importance, in the twentieth century. Caibarién flourished because of the development of the commercial bourgeoisie, while Remedios stagnated.

Caibarién street scene (1930s)
Photo courtesy of Wilder Llanes Méndez

Caibarién street scene (1930s)
Photo courtesy of Wilder Llanes Méndez

PG:
There was a passenger boat, which even Caruso travelled on. He was here. Well, here there were many personalities in the 1930s. It was a golden age. They stayed in the hotel that was near here, the Hotel Internacional. Caibarién had a surprising amount of hotel capacity for the era. And there were many daily services to Havana, with an impressive omnibus company. Plus the sleeping cars, and the boats that left from here.

The Hotel Internacional was the hotel that connected the city with the railway running from the Narcisa sugar mill, travelling along the whole north coast from the east, towards the docks, and western Cuba. Because the city was surrounded by railways.

In 1931, two epic figures of Hispano-American culture passed through Caibarién: Gabriela Mistral, the Chilean poet; and the great Spanish poet, Federico García Lorca. They came to give lectures about their art. I remember that Lorca was returning from Argentina, to New York – the reverse of the journey he had made two years previously.

Steam ship company, Caibarién (1930s)
Photo courtesy of Pedro Manuel González Reinoso

PG:
Lorca was in Caibarién for one day, and gave a lecture near the Hotel Comercio, in the Cervantes Theatre, which had been inaugurated in 1925. The year after its inauguration, in 1926, the great musician from Remedios, Caturla, conducted the local band in Caibarién. Many of the musicians who were in the band went on to become part of the municipal concert band, which was maintained by the Caturla family after 1945.

But the presence of Lorca and Gabriela Mistral in Caibarién gives an idea of how important this municipality was for the cultural life of the country. In the 1930s, the crisis began that ended with the explosion against Machado in 1933. The great Cuban general strike.

Federico García Lorca (left) and Gabriela Mistral (right)

But before that there was a period of splendour for the city. Not just architecturally, but with the intellectual and scientific visits. Other artists passed through here, on their way to Santa Clara, like Caruso, who boarded his ship here. But it is a particular pride for us that García Lorca and Gabriela Mistral stayed here.

Some important composers came out of Caibarién, like Manuel Corona, who was a native. He lived in Havana, but was born here. All his compositions were made here. There were artists like Leopoldo Romañach. The local art gallery still carries his name. Although he wasn't a native of Caibarién (he came from Corralillo), but he moved here, lived much of his life here, and was a famous painter.

Local Caibarién personalities: (L to R) Cartula, Corona, Romañach

However, these golden days for the town did not last. Symbolically, Caibarién was hit by both the hurricane of 1933 and earthquake of 1935. These seemed to mark the start of the protracted decline that the town and its environs suffered over the ensuing years.

OZ:
I think that Caibarién suffered two successive impacts. The first was the general sugar crisis, when sugar expansion was paralysed, related to the Great Depression of 1929, but for particular reasons. That is, there was a saturation of the global sugar market before the 1929 crisis, and the expansion of the Cuban sugar industry ceased. The state established which mills could continue operating, and there were no new zones. It was hardly possible to increase production. Average production in the 1950s was close to the production record of the 1920s. This affected Caibarién, which of course had a second small blow during the Second World War, because during the Second World War in order to combat the activity of German submarines, all sugar exports were concentrated in Havana, and had to leave in convoys, escorted by submarines and warships. And so the small sugar ports stopped operating.

By 1942, with the war taking its effect, not only were the port's activities considerably less than they had been, but Caibarién's chocolate and soap factories had closed, only one banking office remained open, and the sea-going fleet was in tatters. This, combined with the darkening of the coastline for defence reasons, gave the town a very sad appearance. The reversal of fortunes also seemed to be taking its toll on civic life. As the local chronicler commented:

> Social indiscipline has increased, the government of the least capable and administrative robbery. The fine, polished kind of man has been disappearing, drowned by the ordinary and the ungentlemanly. It is a shame that so much good custom, so much respect, order and seriousness, has been lost because of the present domination of so much inept politicking. We have gained materially, but we have gone backwards.

Nevertheless, with the ending of the World War, trade resumed, and although Caibarién never recovered its former glory, commercial life in the town continued in the post-war years.

Caibarién central square (top) and beach (bottom), 1950s
Photos courtesy of Pedro Manuel González Reinoso

PG:
Caibarién was an effervescent port with a promising future. Its golden years of the 1920s and 30s had already passed, but it still had this mercantile flow. Despite the crisis of the 1950s, there was still a noticeable wealthy bourgeoisie here, which was affluent and had an important record of social works and economic progress. This is interesting, because the country in general had declined since 1933.

Advertisement of Caibarién's delights (1950s)
Revista Cayo-Sociales, 1952

> The country was in an absolute crisis. But in the 1950s, the local bourgeoisie sees a rebirth of its hopes, and the notion that we were the centre of the world. In truth, we had some privileges, which other municipalities in the country didn't have. Caibarién could show off some successes, which were isolated, but which made the city a desirable place. Like having magnificent transport. I remember that there were twelve omnibus services a day to Havana. Now there are barely any buses at all.

In 1952, it still seemed possible to describe Caibarién as "the prettiest, cleanest and most attractive city in Cuba" (*Revista Cayo-Sociales*, 1952) – the 'Villa Blanca', with its white buildings. But at the same time, there were clear signs that it had passed its prime. The port urgently needed to be dredged, for example; and there were hopes expressed locally that the building of a viaduct connecting the town to Cayo Conuco and Cayo Francés – where the larger ships had to dock because of the shallowness of Caibarién's waters – would lead to a revitalisation.

> *PG:*
> It was going to have a rail line and a road. It would mean building a causeway with an adjoining railroad, and it would have solved the problem of the barges and all that antiquated marine transportation, what with our bay being too shallow for deep-hulled ships to enter. They had to stay out at Cayo Francés. In order to avoid that, they thought of building the causeway. This was around 1949, in the recession following the World War, and the country thought that this could be ready in the 1950s. But in the end it didn't get made.

The 1959 revolution brought change to Caibarién, as it did throughout Cuba. But in some ways the town was more affected than other places.

> *OZ:*
> The final blow for Caibarién as a sugar port was when after the revolution they developed bulk transport of sugar. So exports became concentrated in those ports in sugar zones with good maritime access, such as Cienfuegos or Nuevitas, which were able to ship in bulk, above all to the markets in eastern Europe and the Soviet Union. So Caibarién practically ceased to operate, apart from some small exports.

Abandoned sugar warehouse, Caibarién (2019)
Photo: Gonzalo Vidal

PG:
As a port on the north coast, dependent upon the historic trade with our neighbour to the north, Caibarién was more affected than, for example, Cuba's southern ports, or even Nuevitas which was the first port to be affected by the end of those trade relations. Trade with the United States ended in a drastic way with the triumph of the revolution.

These were very different times, but despite the changes, life continued in Caibarién, albeit in a more modest way than during its bourgeois heyday.

AAG:
Life was good. We weren't rich, but we had what we needed. We were comfortable, without being well off. I remember that in the 1960s, there was only one television in every block, but there was solidarity. All the children – and there were a lot of us, because of the large demographic explosion that Cuba had – went to those houses, which always opened their doors to all the children of the neighbourhood. One or two of them, no more.

And the same with the fridges. Perhaps there was just one in the whole block, but we all stored our things in that fridge. Everyone volunteered, and nobody charged anything. It was solidarity.

Everything functioned. The sugar factory functioned. The port functioned. The repair workshops functioned. The tannery functioned, despite the sabotage. It still continues to be the largest in the country, now called Patricio Lumumba, although it was regrettably the victim of a counter-revolutionary sabotage in the 1960s. It has been able to recover somewhat, but it never came to recover all that it lost because of that fire.

In 1963, Che opened a bicycle factory – the first and only one that the country had until the 1990s. The revolution had also created a sweet factory, a biscuit factory. And the wages corresponded with the salaries, and the prices corresponded to the wages, and there was work for everyone. And education was and continues to be free. Health as well.

This port that was once famed as a sugar exporter, began to focus more on the other side of its relationship to the sea.

Postcard of the Reforma sugar factory, Caibarién (early 20th century)

Tannery, Caibarién – before 1959 (above), and now (below)
Photos courtesy of Pedro Manuel González Reinoso

OZ:
Caibarién became a fishing port, with variable success – because the fishing from there was also limited.

PG:
There were many fishermen here. Caibarién came to have almost forty fishing platforms – as they called the ferrocement boats which they used for industrial fishing. Each one employed between four and ten workers. Because they were large boats, with cabins, in which they stayed when they went out fishing. They went out for a '*marea*' (tide), which was the name they used, and they would spend a week at sea, and returned laden – because there was an ice factory that functioned, from which they got their supplies.

AAG:
Fish and lobsters were always traditions there. At one time they fished many sponges, of high quality, considered to be amongst the largest in the world in that period.

Fishing boats, Caibarién
Photo courtesy of Pedro Manuel González Reinoso

Lobster boat, Caibarién
Photo courtesy of Pedro Manuel González Reinoso

This was not a new industry. In 1887 there were already 19 fishing boats working with 58 crew, catching almost six thousand sponges. Caibarién gained international fame for this, and this continued into at least the 1960s, after which overfishing and disease brought a sharp decline.

PG:
I remember seeing the docks full of those sponges that were monstrously big, which they cut up with scissors, to make smaller for export.

AAG:
This ended because the sponges are now practically in danger of extinction.

PG:
The sponge gets contaminated with a snail that gets inside, which impedes its development. I saw that once. Somebody explained it to me.

AAG:
It's been years since they extracted any commercially.

PG:
These days I believe that Caibarién has no sponge trade. They aren't even harvested.

Other small industries continued in the aftermath of the revolution.

AAG:
For exports there were the fish that were caught, the lobsters that were found, the sugar – the exports of the sugar derivatives and the treacle that were made in Caibarién. But there was also a pasta factory, a biscuit factory. There was a sweet factory. There were tobacco producers.

Example of a sponge, Museo de las Tradiciones, Caibarién
Image taken from film *Cuba: Living Between Hurricanes*

But sadly, the diversity of Caibarién's economy became slowly restricted – both by commercial pressures, and the policies pursued by the revolutionary government.

> *AOV:*
> After 1959, with the nationalisation of small industries, the mosaic industry in Caibarién ended. Regrettably there was no continuity in the production of that kind of thing.
>
> *PG:*
> My grandfather decided to open a house-rental agency and dry cleaners, where my family lived until 1968, when it was closed by the famous revolutionary offensive.

Life changed after 1959, in many ways for the better, but also accompanied by a feeling of chronic shortage that has not gone away since.

> *AAG:*
> I remember that as a child, there was a shortage of sweets in the sweet shop, of drinks in the bars, the sugary refreshing drinks, also rum, cigarettes, tobacco. But not meat nor other products that came rationed through the ration books, which were enough to live decently. Those were not lacking. There was a shortage of clothes, a shortage of accessories, a shortage of make-up. Jewellery. But not in what was essential.
>
> And above all, the country counted on the general support of its people, because we felt that we were protagonists in this history, and we were prepared to face up to whatever was necessary. I remember that there were children who went to school without shoes, or missing a shoe, or a shoe of one colour and one of another colour, or two from the same foot. But nobody ever made fun of them. On the contrary, if a child was sick, all the others would take a tin of condensed milk from their personal allowance, so that the child could have some extra food. The teachers were very concerned about their pupils.
>
> We lived that great solidarity. Milk bottles were left outside the doors, and nobody took them. If children left their toys lying around, they were still wherever they had dropped them.

I remember that one day I went to the library by bicycle, at three in the afternoon. I read some books, and when I left I forgot the bicycle. A few days later, when I was thinking about going to the library: where's the bike? I went, and after nearly seventy hours, the bicycle was right there. Nobody had taken it. If it was very hot, you opened the door to the street. You felt perfectly safe. And there was, above all, a spirit of solidarity in the town.

The revolution brought with it new allies and economic partners, with the Soviet Union and the socialist bloc, and this led to sugar continuing to be the country's primary export.

HV:
After the triumph of the Cuban revolution, sugar continued to predominate. What happened is that the market changed. For practically the remainder of the twentieth century, sugar changed its market towards the socialist countries, those of Comecon.

OZ:
Cuban sugar production continued increasing at a time when production was practically paralysed throughout the Caribbean area – and even disappeared, as in the case of Puerto Rico. This was because of the connection with the Soviet market, and of the other European socialist countries. As a result, while under capitalism, in the 1950s, the average sugar harvest was around five million tons; in the 1980s, it was around eight million tons. There was a notable increase. This occurred on the basis of the preferential prices that the Soviets paid.

The Cuban industry grew during the 1970s and 1980s. It had become mechanised, above all because of the exceptionally elevated prices that the Soviet Union paid. Which was not out of charity, but because the cost of producing beet sugar in the Soviet Union was very high; and so even when they bought Cuban sugar for three, four or even five times the price of sugar on the world market, it was a good deal for them, because Cuba converted the income from its sugar account with the Soviet Union into oil and machinery. So it was was an economic relationship that was convenient for both parties.

For a while, this helped to maintain Caibarién's economy. But with the increasing size of transport vessels, the port wasn't in a position to keep up with demand.

PG:
Caibarién as a port survived while the socialist bloc lasted, with ships coming from there. First they stopped in Nuevitas, and afterwards in Caibarién, to then continue towards Matanzas and then Havana. These were the northern ports that were key for enabling transportation within the internal economy. At these places merchandise arrived, and was taken to the most important production centres in the provinces.

But it was the port of Cienfuegos that was the large port, responsible for almost all the progress in the centre of the island for strategic reasons. Cienfuegos Bay has all the necessary conditions. It's deep, which is not the case here. Mariel is the same, Matanzas is the same. But Caibarién does not have the necessary depth.

AAG:
We lived beyond our economic means. The socio-economic system was not so efficient nor well administered, but we had a bit of help from the Soviet Union and the socialist countries. And that occurred because we lived beyond our economic means. We lived beyond what we produced. And the state had very paternalist policies, with a lot of free things, many free things. And generally that's why in the 1960, 70s and especially the 80s, we lived splendidly.

There were difficult patches. In 1969, 1970, with the campaign for the Ten Million Ton sugar harvest. Sugar prices rose on the world market, and they wanted to have an enormous sugar harvest in order to finance the technical foundation of a developed socialist society. And there was a big endeavour. I remember that 1969 was the 'Year of the Decisive Effort', and 1970 was the 'Year of the Ten Million'. The whole country concentrated on the sugar industry. In fact there were other areas of the economy that weren't well looked after because of the focus on sugar. And a record harvest was achieved. But we didn't reach ten million, and that, naturally, was a burden for the economy. Sugar prices fell, and although eight and a half million tons were produced, which was a record, the country entered into a crisis.

But although times may not have been easy, the close relationship with the Soviet Union and the socialist bloc brought a measure of economic security. However, with the collapse of the Soviet Union in 1991, the whole of Cuba was plunged into a deep economic crisis. Communities like Caibarién appeared particularly precarious in the new conditions.

PG:
What happened is that when trade with the eastern socialist bloc ended in the 1990s, we found ourselves with a complete lack of employment. All the small ports of Cuba closed.

OZ:
When the Soviet Union disappeared, and the preferential market for Cuban sugar disappeared, Cuba had to turn to the international sugar market. The world market is a residual market, because most sugar that is traded internationally, is traded within preferential markets. That is to say, that in the free market you have to accept lower prices.

So Cuba had to sell its sugar at a price that could be three times less than what it was being sold at two years previously, with production costs that were increasing. But production was maintained largely because it was the only source of income that the country had. But while the 1989/90 harvest was in the region of eight million tons, in 1994 only four million tons were produced. Why? Because fertilisers had disappeared, because fuel to power the turbines to move water for irrigation had disappeared. So cane yields, which were approximately 60 tons per hectare, fell to 30 tons, and sometimes less than 30. There started to be a shortage of cane. And it was difficult to maintain and replace the equipment in the sugar factories. So by the end of the 1990s, of the 154 sugar centrals existing on the island, probably there were already 50 that were not operating, because they weren't in condition to do so.

Caibarién's only sugar mill, the Marcelo Salado – which had been founded in 1859, originally as the Lapeyre (surname of the family that owned it), but later becoming the Reforma – was one of those that ended production. However, it has subsequently been granted a fresh lease of life, functioning now as a sugar museum. This has brought some measure of continuity to the town – which anyway had always had a more diverse economy. Other former sugar communities around the island, particularly those that were wholly dependent upon this for their livelihoods, have not been so fortunate. This is true not so far from Caibarién: elsewhere in the Remedios area former sugar factories have also been forced to close – such as the José María Pérez (formerly Fe) in Camajuaní, the Luis Arcos Bergnes (formerly Carmita) in Vueltas, the Carbó Serviá (formerly Fidencia) in Placetas, or the Narcisa in Yaguajay.

AVE:
I think it is important to begin talking about how life in the sugar towns changed after the mills closed. You feel the impact when you have known a place with all its social and cultural life, and you arrive back there and all that you find are skeletal structures and a few pieces of masonry converted into family homes. It left me feeling frozen inside, because it is such a strong impact. Finding that there is nothing left.

Remains of the Narcisa sugar factory, Yaguajay (2010)
Photo: Wilder Llanes Méndez

Overgrown buildings of former Fidencia sugar mill, Placetas (2018)
Photo: Ana Vera Estrada

> Everything changed very rapidly, and that is at the root of the errors that were committed when the state told the workers to begin the demolition and process the equipment that could be extracted or reused from these deconstructed sugar factories, in order to reinsert them in the sugar economy or other industries. There was a lot of confusion, and really a terrible administration of the salvaged resources that were sold or passed over to other institutions or other sugar factories, or other workshops, or even to private individuals.
>
> In general, you could say that the majority of the people affected faced the situation with suffering – a suffering out of which they didn't emerge, because they were facing a premature end of their working life. Often, because of the absence of options, they were given the possibility of taking early retirement, and many did. While that was a suffering they didn't come out of, they gradually did emerge through their children, when they were able to leave to take up different positions in the new tourist economy, or other production. While the young people also suffered, they hadn't participated in the building of the factory, and so their pain was less.

In such communities, those previously involved in the sugar industry are having to find alternatives, which all too often have not been readily available.

AVE:
There were some opportunities, but very few. There was a small private sector, but I didn't see any dynamism there for the creation of small businesses, in the tertiary market. There was very little, almost none. Gastronomy, almost nothing. And a lot of emigration. Emigration out of the country. The people didn't lose their houses. They remained living there, but working in other places that were more or less close. But all the transport had been connected to the factory, and when that went, local transportation disappeared. So they had to arrange other ways for getting to work.

It is difficult to make generalisations, but some women tended to remain in work related to food, to making small things for selling from a stall on a corner. The women tended towards that, to domestic work. But the men quickly inserted themselves as, for example, builders, barbers, drivers. There were some jobs that were for men.

How did people feel about the closure of the sugar factory? It is a pain that is still latent in the people who live in those places. They are places with few people living, with serious housing problems, with housing that has been improvised with pieces of masonry from the factories, or in the connected offices. People who despite not being overly old, have been unable to insert themselves in any way into a smaller economy.

However, for many the opportunity has been given for turning to agriculture, on the lands that were formerly devoted to sugarcane.

AVE:
There was a return to the land, with the opening up of options for renting state lands that had previously been dedicated to cane, and which supposedly had to be changed to food production to meet local necessities. Not really for export outside the municipality.

I interviewed a man who was working a small vegetable patch. He told me that he had finally graduated as an engineer aged 60, fulfilling his lifelong dream, because he had never had time nor education to finish his studies. Of course now there wasn't any kind of work available for him – until he turned 65, and could take his pension. A university graduate who had no way of reinserting himself in the economy.

Local produce market, Caibarién (2019)
Image taken from film *Cuba: Living Between Hurricanes*

Cuba has invested a great deal in raising the educational level of the people, but the changed economic reality has left many highly qualified people unable to work in their chosen profession, facing an uncertain future.

AVE:
There was a significant amount of technical potential there. Young people who had graduated from specialist schools, who had concentrated all their effort in preparing themselves for specialist work in the sugar industry. When the sugar industry disappeared, some became self-employed and so went to clear land that had belonged to the state, but which was now covered in sicklebush. And they devoted themselves to growing fruit and vegetables.

Going from being a sugar worker, to being an agricultural worker, and living in a rural community that supposedly has a guaranteed water service, transport service, but only the minimum. Not like it was in times of the sugar factory, which carried all the cost. From the point of view of these people, it hasn't been something they chose, but rather was something they encountered.

AVE:
They didn't make a decision to change. They were fine how they were. They had everything subsidised, and the state couldn't continue subsidising that. They didn't only subsidise the oil that was used to operate the mill, but they also subsidised the transport, they subsidised the water for the houses, the electricity, the telephone, the medical service. This was all subsidised. And they would open the taps, and the water would be left running for the whole day. They didn't have to pay. The same with the electricity. Everything was subsidised. The same with any problem of breakage in the house. Broken kitchen stoves, broken motorcycle – everything was taken to the factory to find a solution. In carpentry, building, whatever. Help from the Central. That is to say that the Central was also a leak. It was a leaking colander, because the budget of the sugar central was lost in many ways. The workers' snacks ended up in the houses of the employees who distributed the food.

The 'Special Period' of the 1990s was far more devastating than any hurricane could ever be. Its effects were felt acutely in Caibarién – as, of course, they were throughout Cuba.

Abandoned boat and dock, Caibarién (present day)
Photo: Pedro Manuel González Reinoso

Caibarién fishing port (2018)
Aerial photograph by Ariel Suárez, courtesy of Giselle García Castro

AAG:
The town changed following the fall of the Berlin Wall, and the disappearance of the Soviet Union two years later. In the catastrophic collapse of the economy, the deep recession that fell over the country, I went for ten years without being able to go to Caibarién because of the transport problems.

With the collapse of much of the town's economic infrastructure, attempts to continue activities – even those that were so important for local life, like fishing – were difficult.

PG:
Now the ice that is made is minimal, and they sell that ice to the fishermen so that they can go out on their very small *mareas*, of just two or three days. They can't do more, because they don't have any way of preserving the fish. The fish decomposes very easily, and there is the risk of causing a massive intoxication. So the *mareas* are very short, just two or three days.

PG:
In Cuba, the fishing fleet was extinguished – at least the Atlantic fishing fleet. Large trawlers don't exist anymore. Now there are small shrimping boats and trawlers, but not the fishing fleet there once was. And there are still those sporting boats, which have an agreement with the state. They extract fish as self-employed, and sell it to the fishing company that processes it.

So what Caibarién primarily does, as these are all of different species – we're not talking about a school of fish of the same kind that can be marketable – is to pick out the largest, the best, and these are filleted. They are used for certain purposes, above all for sale to the tourist sector. And the rest is processed as mixed meat, as a mince, and it is sold to the people. Luckily the industrial fishing company has a kind of small stall from which it sells a part of this to the people. For example, sardines for feeding animals and people. Many people have domestic animals that need to be fed, and so they go there to get this fish. And the rest is sold in processed form. They make fish sausages, fish fillets, or things like that. But it is a reduced amount, just for local provision.

Thankfully the company managed to separate itself from the provincial institution. Almost all the fish from there used to go to Santa Clara, and the town didn't see any of it.

Symbolic of how Caibarién has fallen on hard times, and emblematic of the country's general loss of connections, the railway lines that at one time had linked the town to the rest of Cuba, and had brought so much wealth through, are now abandoned – the station empty and the tracks overgrown.

But slowly efforts are being made to rebuild the town, from the combined ravages of economic decline and impact of hurricanes.

AOV:
Fortunately today, with the recovery of local industry, with the recovery of what is the best heritage from the past, there has been a return, a revitalisation of the mosaic industry. We have discovered producers who, despite the passage of time, have connected with the past, and are making these again.

Caibarién railway station today (2019)
Photos: Gonzalo Vidal

PG:
Almost every family in Caibarién has a representative across the sea. For us, 'across the sea' means Florida, or rather Miami or Tampa, those regions in the south of the United States where there are always natives of Caibarién. It's rarer to find any in Spain, but there are some. They have also gone to Spain, because the nationality laws have given them the possibility of travelling to Europe.

Whether through remittances of funds and other resources from family and friends living abroad, or the return to Caibarién of those who had previously either emigrated or travelled to work in other countries – individual architectural improvements can be seen around the town.

AAG:
People have begun to fix their houses. But sometimes without any sense of order. I remember the homogeneity of those porches and those wooden houses. Today that has been messed up: a house here, another there. The eaves at different heights. More solid, stronger, more resistant to hurricanes, but without harmony.

Roof repairing, Caibarién (2019)
Photo: Gonzalo Vidal

PG:
Because the repairs being carried out in Caibarién have been urgent, they have been made without the necessary resources, using building materials that aren't lasting. A metallic roof fixed with screws might resist some of the time, but won't resist the wind; and the walls, built quickly in contaminated areas, with low quality cement. Also the pragmaticism of the builders. Almost always the houseowners have thrown themselves into the task, and have put up walls without the supervision of an architect. Although there are architects – the community is obliged to consult them. But they do so in an almost automatic fashion: "Ah, yes, I've checked it. So I'll sign the paper, because it's your wall. If it falls, then it's your problem" – because it will fall on you one day.

There are still houses in Caibarién that were damaged by Kate, and haven't recovered. Almost 34 years later. If there is another storm, I'm crossing my fingers that we don't have to leave Caibarién, those who still remain. The city isn't in condition to withstand strong winds like those again. It might not all collapse, but the damage is going to be greater.

Examples of new private constructions, Caibarién (2019) (above and opposite)
Photos: Gonzalo Vidal

5 Environmental Changes

What is certain is that we are heading towards an impoverishment of the environmental system, if we don't detain all these poisoning processes.

Pedro Manuel González Reinoso

Throughout Cuba, the economic developments of the past two centuries in particular have taken their toll on the environment.

RF:
Sugar completely transformed the Cuban landscape. Before sugar, cattle or other crops. In mountainous zones, coffee. But sugar was the principal factor for the transformation of the landscape, and of deforestation in Cuba.

Historically, much of Cuba had been covered by forests. It has been estimated that at the time of Spanish conquest, as much as 90 percent of the island's surface was woodland – three-quarters of which was tropical, and the rest made up of pines and low-lying cover. This proved to be a very useful resource, with the Spanish state protecting the forests, and harvesting the precious woods they contained in a managed way. Cuban trees went to build many of the ships in the Spanish fleet. The region of Remedios,

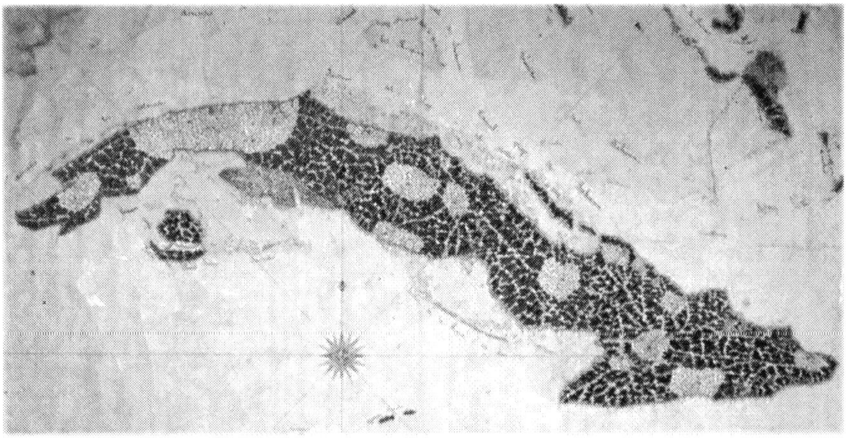

Map of Cuba showing woodland (1816)
Map by H. Boyon (Museo Naval, Madrid), courtesy of Reinaldo Funes Monzote

where Caibarién is situated, was an important zone for such logging, and was considered to have abundant wood of all classes available.

By the beginning of the nineteenth century, large patches in the island's forest cover had opened up. But other than in the more agriculturally developed area around Havana and Matanzas – which was already almost entirely denuded – most of Cuba still retained much of its woodland, as can be seen in contemporary maps.

But as the sugar frontier implacably extended down the island during the nineteenth century, most of these forests were lost.

RF:
The splendour of the sugar industry depended upon the devastation, the destruction of the forests. For three fundamental reasons: for the wood, obviously for the infrastructure; for the fuel; and, above all, for the fertility of the soils. That is, in the whole of this region, sugar was established, but after thirty or forty years the mills began to abandon the land in order to expand the sugar frontier. And that sugar frontier, of course, came with the cost of an environmental transformation, the transformation of the forests, and the whole of this region in that period. The forests were destroyed to grow cane, and extract immediate benefits. That was the tendency, practically up to the beginning of the twentieth century.

The Remedios area experienced the full brunt of this deforestation in the second half of the nineteenth century, as large sugar plantations came to dominate much of the land. While in 1862, 78 percent was still woodland, by 1899 this had plummeted to just 12 percent. Although initially the clearing of forests provided very rich soil for planting, with intensive cultivation this could not last.

> *RF:*
> When the great forests were gone, that organic mass of the soil, the yields from the cane started to fall, and the only way to maintain an acceptable or profitable level of production was the option of industrialising the agricultural sector. That is, they started by industrialising the manufacturing side: the steam engines, the centrifuge, and all that machinery, including the railways, which was central. But afterwards, from the Second World War, the rural sector begins to be modernised, with the massive introduction of mechanisation, of tractors, of lorries. Lorries begin to replace the railways. The application of ever greater amounts of agro-chemicals begins, especially after the revolution; as well as irrigation. Without these three factors, it wouldn't have been possible to maintain the relative development of the sugar industry into the 1990s.

Such effects can be seen in and around Caibarién, where the impact of uncontrolled exploitation of resources has left the land damaged and polluted.

> *AM:*
> The sugar industry left its mark. The worst that I know of is the River Guaní, which is the channel that the Heriberto Duquesne sugar factory used as an outflow for all the residues of sugar production and the distilling of alcohol. The must that there is in that river is almost a metre deep, or more. It has practically done away with all the fauna, in the riverbed, and the fishes. You can't now walk beside the river. It's a disaster. We used to think that the edges of the river bank would be one of the most important archaeological zones that we have, since of course the precolumbian peoples generally settled near to sources of water. At that time, the river must have been very pretty, with a strong flow. However, we could never find anything along the riverbanks, because it was so difficult to walk there due to the man-made damage that exists there.

PG:
The flow of the River Guaní has been contaminated by all the waste from the Chiquitico Fabregat and Duquesne sugar factories, in the area of Buenavista. The river flows down from those heights, and the tributaries have been polluted with the must that is derived from the manufacture of the final syrups that they use to distil the alcohol from which they make the famous rums that come from here, known as Mulata. This river flows into Buenavista Bay, and this has been contaminating the zone over many years – since the period in which those mills were founded [in the nineteenth century]. And as a result, it has become impossible to make use of the stream to irrigate, or to feed animals, because they could be poisoned.

Mulata rum label

The polluted Guaní River (2019)
Photos: Pedro Manuel González Reinoso

PG:
When the intense period of the sugar harvest comes to an end, the river clears a bit. It stops having that must, but is bad smelling, dragging all that has been feeding the banks with germs towards Buenavista Bay – which is a UNESCO-protected biosphere, but is profoundly contaminated by all this waste that doesn't stop.

It is not only the water that has been adversely affected by intensive sugar cultivation and production. The land as well has suffered a long-term impact.

AM:
There has been damage done to the soil due to the growing of sugar-cane. The use of fertilisers and bactericides and all those things that were good for the cane, but not for the cultivation of other crops. And this also produced the degradation of the soil in cane-growing zones.

Throughout the Cuban countryside, the effects of this can be seen

Invasive sicklebush (marabú – Dichrostachys cinerea)
Photo: Ramiro Chaves

– symbolised by the spread of invasive plants, in particular the sicklebush, or *marabú*, where productive crops once grew.

> *AM:*
> In all those cane zones that were deactivated, that were completely eliminated as sugarcane plantations, the sicklebush has overgrown, because it is a very resistant plant and all that chemical damage suffered by the soil didn't harm it.
>
> *PG:*
> The sacks of fertiliser were piled up along the cane-field boundaries. There were fertilisers that were nitrogenated, and they were used almost indiscriminately on those lands so that the sugarcane would grow rapidly. And one might ask, how much of this nitrogen was going to go into the rest of the produce. It is very painful to see the impact on the soil. The earth is fumigated with pesticides, and fertilised with nitrogen-based chemicals, which gradually poisons the fertile topsoil. This has been happening over too many years. It's still being done in some zones.

Although historically the sugar agro-industrial complex has probably been responsible for most of the problems of environmental damage and pollution, it is by no means the only culprit. The Remedios area has long been an important zone for the cultivation of tobacco, in particular in the vicinity of Vueltas and Camajuaní.

> *PG:*
> The tobacco industry has had a similar effect. It needs too many chemical products to preserve the tobacco growth. So, an enormous quantity of pesticides and fungicides are applied.
>
> *RF:*
> Also cattle ranching. Many places had some kind of treatment, but they often didn't work well. They weren't maintained. This shows that there was knowledge of the problem, but often the cattle economy did not allow it to be prioritised, beyond the plans for annual growth, and the maintenance of production. The fulfilling of export contracts, etcetera.

Cattle near Caibarién (2019)

Image taken from film *Cuba: Living Between Hurricanes*

Intensive agricultural exploitation of the land over the past two centuries has resulted in the once fertile soils becoming seriously degraded in many places.

AM:
Around Remedios there are rocky outcrops in the ground. This is natural. It is a geological process which manifests itself in this way, with outcrops of rocks. But at the same time, the soil has been degraded. It is being washed away, by the rainstorms that are sometimes torrential. And as there is no effective control of drainage for these waters, they flow freely, and drag the sediment towards the sea. The soil is lost, and those limestone formations are exposed.

PG:
The majority of those soils that were at one time dedicated to sugarcane agriculture, were then converted either into pasture for animals that have become increasingly scarce, or in terrain for varied cultivations – but are already damaged.

This compounds the impact of weather, especially when there is an oscillation between drought and extreme events such as hurricanes.

MN:
When there is no plant coverage, if there is large-scale precipitation, it clears the soil that has no protective covering. Certainly there are programmes for protection and avoiding salinisation and deterioration of the soils, as is logical. But this does have a negative impact, especially here in the coastal zone, with the danger of salt intrusion which also contributes to the loss of soil. Not just drought. In years that are very dry, and the aquifers diminish, measures are taken to pump drinking water less frequently for the population, to avoid the water table decreasing, and to avoid the sea intruding along the coastal zones.

Caibarién is increasingly suffering from a combination of problems caused by both problematic drainage, and contamination of the water supply.

RF:
In this zone, for example, I realised that there had been many problems with drainage. If you look at a map of Cuba, in the whole of this region, the north of Las Villas, there are many drainage works: channels that were opened at one moment or another in order to avoid the flooding of the land, of these soils.

PG:
Those channels have become underutilised with the passage of time, and are practically disused. They only function when there are natural floods, to hold back the sea. Evidently the owners of sugar mills in these areas decided to shift the land use towards other crops.

Industrial activity in Caibarién – both the production of leather and the processing of fish – has compounded the environmental problems now being faced.

PG:
The sugar industry utilises a series of harmful chemicals for the clarification, the sugarcane liquor and everything; but they aren't as harmful as those used in the curing of leather. They combine in the water, resulting in the massive poisoning of the river.

PG:
For many years the tanning industry in Caibarién has produced a kind of permanent pollution in the air that we breathe. When the tannery was at its height, there was an oxidation lagoon, which emitted gases, affecting us with a smell of burnt chicken feathers. You know that in the making of leathers, they use hundreds of chemical products that were poured into that lagoon. Whenever there is a period of intense rain, the oxidation lagoon overflows, and flows towards the sea.

Likewise, there is the case of the fish-processing plant, which was never finished, so they continue to tip their waste into the sea. For the past thirty years they have been throwing out the waste from the processing and the conservation of supplies (the chlorine and all the other substances used for freezing), into the sea. There is a recycling plant that was bought four years ago, but which hasn't been able to operate because it lacks parts that have to be bought in Peru, using Japanese technology. They have been announcing that it is going to start functioning, but still we continue throwing the waste from the food industry into the sea.

While on the one hand, Caibarién – as with much of Cuba, and indeed the world – has to find a way of dealing with, and overcoming, years of misuse and lack of awareness of the environmental damage being caused by industry and human settlement; on the other, global climate change is further increasing the dangers faced.

MN:
I have been working for seventeen years in the meteorological station, and the question of global warming has always piqued my curiosity. Ever since the 1950s or 1960s, global warming and climate change has been spoken about.

LER:
In Cuba, the state decided to begin studies to observe if climate change was occurring in Cuba. In the 1990s, the Cuban Academy of Sciences told the Institute of Meteorology and other institutions in the country to carry out a study that would reveal if these changes, if global warming, was occurring or not.

From that they derived the first extensive scientific study to try to clarify what was happening. And since then, work has been carried out in Cuba, alongside the Intergovernmental Panel on Climate Change (an initiative of the United Nations in cooperation with almost all the countries in the world), and other studies have been completed in the country that have resulted in periodic communications. This is led by the Ministry of Science, Technology and the Environment (CITMA), its environment agency, and many other institutions. This is to keep the state up-to-date, and for its institutions to keep the general public informed about how these changes are developing.

MN:
I decided to make an analysis of the data series that we have accumulated. The station has an effective circular range of ten kilometres. We have been able to prove that from the 1950s to the first decade of the twenty-first century, for example, the minimum temperature has risen by 1.9°, the average maximum by 0.8° and the maximum by 0.9°. The wind speeds have slightly risen. The temperature at ten in the evening has increased with respect to previous years. Then the daytime heat has extended into the night, just as summer has extended into winter. Also precipitation, although the changes haven't been perceptible, have shown a very small difference. That is to say, I consider that it is real that we are in the presence of a global warming that is provoking climate change on a global level.

However, there is some disagreement amongst experts as to the extent that this is being felt.

LER:
The climate statistics do not show such a big difference. What does appear is that the minimum overnight temperatures used to be a bit lower than they are now. But the maximums are roughly the same. More or less. I don't think there has been such a difference. In the nineteenth century and the start of the twentieth, they would say to the children and the young people, don't go out onto the street at midday, because it might harm you. And it's true, because of the sun, and when you sweat you might dehydrate. You feel bad. Your blood pressure goes down. You lose potassium.

Whatever may be happening with temperatures, it seems undeniable that the sea level is rising, and coastal communities such as Caibarién are already feeling the effects of this.

MN:
According to marinographers in Isabela de Sagua, since the 1980s it has been shown that the sea levels are rising for two fundamental reasons: the increase in the volume caused by expansion, due to the heat; and the contribution of freshwater coming from the melting of ice. Here in north-central Cuba, it is rising by a millimetre each year. Which is to say that since then, it has increased by two or three centimetres. Imperceptible to the human eye, but it really has an impact on the whole of a town like this, with its drainage difficulties.

AM:
There is evidence in Caibarién of the rise in the sea level, caused by climate change. Because I've seen it. And I've consulted with people who are a lot older than me, who have lived their whole lives in the area of the Malecón, where I live, and there has never been anything like it. And here it is felt more, because this is a shallow bay with a lot of muddy sediment.

Flooding in Caibarién (2018)
Photo: Pedro Manuel González Reinoso

And now we are seeing, now I've noticed that the high tides are now invading zones of the city: there on the Malecón, near to where I live. The marine flow now penetrates through the town's drainage channels, and starts to flood those low parts. This didn't use to happen. I've talked with people, fishermen, old people who have been living for eighty or ninety years in Caibarién, and this situation has never happened before. Nevertheless, now it is. The sea level due to climate change is now having its effect in Caibarién. Now the sea is penetrating, even sometimes at high tide despite there being no wind, and there is no meteorological phenomenon.

A large quantity of sediments is accumulating along the coasts, caused by this rise in the sea level, and the waves are having more effect. The high tides are higher. And there is seabed erosion occurring, with all this being dumped on the shore.

Caibarién is amongst the seventy Cuban coastal populations that are going to be most affected. In fact, it is amongst the twenty coastal locations suffering the greatest effects, within a period of fifty to eighty years. This isn't thousands of years, nothing like that, but rather decades, so any young person now will experience the impact of the rising sea level. More than 30 percent of Caibarién's coast is going to disappear in a matter of decades. Perhaps a hundred years.

The effects of these changes are already increasingly being felt by the inhabitants of Caibarién.

PG:
In the farm where I used to work, there were wells from which the municipality of Caibarién got its drinking water. They were wells with crystal-clear water, from springs. Caibarién's aqueduct made use of gravity, bringing the water down from the hills of Buenavista and Carrillo. And that was subterranean water. It's not the water that we drink today, which comes from the water table that has been contaminated by the sea, and for that reason it is salty. Because of the pollution, the climate change, the rising tide – all that has combined to modify the infrastructure of the water table. My father was an agronomic engineer, and he worked in irrigation. He warned about the salinisation of the wells.

MN:
All this – climate change, the rise in sea level – contributes to the more dangerous elements of cyclones or hurricanes having a strong effect on the coastal population. Why? Because when the sea penetrates, it is difficult to get rid of the water, because it has to be recognised that the state of housing of the population is not always very good. And with regular or bad housing, there is greater vulnerability to strong winds. Which is why houses collapse, totally or partially, roofs get lost. And then with the rising sea level, the slope of the land is not sufficient, as the velocity of the drainage waters meets the barrier of the sea.

Rising sea levels continue to compound the already existing problems of water pollution and inadequate drainage.

PG:
Caibarién's waste goes in two directions. One ends up in the sea, which is the most serious, because though the sea seems to be a great recycler, it isn't. What it does in the end is transform the waste into another kind of ecological damage. And the other goes inland, like for example when people travelling on the roads throw out cans, or throw their garbage into the rivers – which are also tributaries of the sea, in the end.

The whole town has an archaic system of drainage that flows out into the sea. The drainage of the city was designed to work through gravity. With the sea level rising, and the population growing, there isn't the necessary drainage system here. I made a small study for *Guardabosques* concerning the sewage and the drinking water supply. Caibarién's mains water pipes are constructed from iron, and they are laid underground. The joints were soldered with lead, which is highly toxic. This is still there, in the soil, from all those pipes, perhaps as much as a result of the seismic vibrations as of their structure itself. When they installed the Crucero water tower, all these tubes couldn't withstand the pressure of the water, and they burst. That's why you see the streets flooded, because there is a considerable loss of drinking water, which is being pumped and pumped, and doesn't reach the houses because the water infrastructure is very weak, precarious, very old, and needs to be replaced.

It is worrying to see the contamination in the drainage channels. Not so much of sewage, as of waste from the nearby houses. There are zones where the people are also dumping their waste directly into the sea. It is very sad to go out on a boat and see all the waste that neighbours thrown not into the rubbish bins, but into the sea. And then in revenge the sea returns this to us.

If you go through the new neighbourhood that was recently opened, you will see how all the streets have the same problem of flooding as these ones – and the neighbourhood hasn't been open for even a decade. Why? Because they did not design the drainage system so that it would be adequate for the number of people who they were expecting to live there. The pipes aren't big enough to take all the sewage water and residue from these neighbourhoods, and so it overflows into the streets. There's even a neighbourhood that was finished a year and a half ago, and they couldn't hand it over because they didn't include drainage for the residual water. Who are the people in charge, who should have foreseen this?

Polluted drainage channel, Caibarién (2018)
Photo: Pedro Manuel González Reinoso

Local environmental activists report on the worst examples of ecological decay, and its impact on the community, through unofficial channels, such as *Guardabosques* – a national network of environmental campaigners, seeking to draw both public and official attention to the problems being faced, and the need for improvement. In the February 2019 edition of the organisation's publication, the Caibarién resident, Pedro Manuel González Reinoso, reported on what he described as 'Lost Time':

> It hurts to see these images now, months after writing the report that I never published. In Caibarién we were in a drought, watching the community-sector engineers carrying out works over several months in 2018. 'Aqueduct workers', they said. Out of pity and consideration for those honest working fellows, who could not (or didn't want to) do the job well, I abstained from revealing what occurred at that moment. And also for the enthusiastic neighbours who accompanied them, even helping to carry pipes, to install the new mains valve that took a hell of a lot of effort (and money) to obtain from the tight-fisted military – since there's rarely a hope that they might hand over their 'material destined for the development of tourism' (by which those in their ranks survive). A thousand obstacles.

Drainage problems in Caibarién (2018) (this page and opposite)
Photos: Pedro Manuel González Reinoso

Few people now care that the water bubbles out of the battered former fountain of eternal decrepitude that we denounced in this journal some years ago. Emblem that welcomes with its humidifying atmosphere all visitors that arrive in our now arid town (as if to muddy its heraldic device); right by the gates to the zoo, which is another unspeakable environmental disaster.

I maintained the foolish hope that this time the repair would work and last, and that we would not keep pouring away water, which has been escaping through the collimated joints of the pipes of my town, thanks to the efforts of the lorries overladen with weights that are inappropriate for our venerable streets.

For at least a century the whole water network has been buried, constructed with archaic technology from other eras. Made from cast iron, with very worn connectors, that were thought to be everlasting, sealed with a solvent derived from poisonous lead. As a boy I remember the smell floating around the housing blocks, as they smelted bullion bars of heavy metal. Since then that method is no longer used, but they continue there, beneath the ground. Highly dangerous lead, that releases invisible ions every time the water passes (when it passes). And it reaches our thirsty mouths, unaware of the mixture that we are swallowing.

I look at yesterday's work; at the street that has been broken and mended a thousand times. When they turn the water back on, without a doubt, the avenue will be flooded. At the same time, many trees will grow in the midst

Drainage problems in Caibarién (2018)
Photos: Pedro Manuel González Reinoso

of such waste, the mosquitos will flourish, we will have more dengue. We persevere, in a cyclical and interminable way, like in the work of Marcel Proust, in search of lost time.

It is impossible to visit Caibarién, and not be struck by the consequences of poor drainage, visible in the streets.

AAG:
Caibarién's drains have always been precarious. Because of the construction carried out voluntarily by homeowners, the channels became closed. They blocked them and nobody worried about it. And naturally, that affected the traditional drainage system, and the flooding in Caibarién is constant. The mosquitos are constant. And so I see everything heading in that direction.

PG:
I have seen dead animals. I see them coming out of the drainage channels all the time. They end up on the Malecón. The water becomes unbearable because of the stench of these decomposing bodies. There are people who have constructed cesspits in their homes, without permission, with overflow into the sea. And right now there is a real danger in swimming in the waters of the bay – something that I used to do when I was a boy. I was born on the Malecón, when the Malecón was just a small stretch of two blocks. Not like now that it has all been built up: something that took twenty years to finish, the same as the Giza Pyramid. And when they opened it, we thought that it would put an end to these undesirable tributes offered to the sea. But that's not what happened.

Also, there is waste that through various routes reaches the beach from Buenavista. It makes the water turbid, lacking in transparency. The spread of algae, which used to be much less, and the upsurge of jellyfish. The medusas that tend to arrive in Cuba towards the end of summer, in August or September, are a danger for everyone, because firstly they cause a rash on contact, and then they infect the whole shoreline with their decomposition, because they die. They don't live long, and when they die they fill the shore with their dead bodies. This has unfortunately been increasing for years.

Polluted coastline, Caibarién (2018)
Photo: Pedro Manuel González Reinoso

PG:
There are campsites and hotels that tip their wastewater directly into the sea nearby. The hotel that is on the beach doesn't have a cess pit, a sewer. Rather it has a pipeline, dating from when it was built in the twentieth century, that goes under the water, and in the middle of the bay, about thirty metres from the shore, you can see how all the waste comes out of the pipe. I personally investigated it, with a mask and flippers. When I was younger, back when the water was clearer (because now you can't see it because the water is so turbid), you could see the pipe, which was mysterious to me. And so I investigated, and they told me that it was the pipeline through which the hotel poured its wastewater into the sea. But it isn't far from the shore, and continues functioning like that, because the hotel doesn't have separate drainage.

What is certain is that we are heading towards an impoverishment of the environmental system, if we don't detain all these poisoning processes.

Of course, all this is not only having a serious impact on the human environment, but can be felt in other species that depend upon the local ecosystem.

AM:
I am very observant. I have noticed several things that are related to the changes in the ecosystem, because of the problem of global warming and, well, other things. In Caibarién you practically no longer hear the singing of frogs when it rains. In Caibarién you don't hear the frogs sing. It's incredible. They have disappeared. But what happened? Either there are very few, or none.

The effect on the migration of birds from North America can be seen. I have noticed that in recent years there has been little. You don't see those large flocks of birds that used to come here from the north. This has diminished enormously. The multitudes, the enormous flocks of swallows, of domestic birds, of bats, are now, while not non-existent, certainly very scarce.

Algae-infested coast, Caibarién (2019)
Photo: Gonzalo Vidal

PG:
As a native of Caibarién, I have also felt the absence of the migration of crustaceans. It worries me a lot that one of the symbols of this municipality are the crabs that have disappeared, slowly, from the scene. The same is happening with marine crustaceans, not only land crabs. The ancient migrations of crabs (*jaibas*), because the territory used to be crossed by them every year from one side to the other. That has disappeared.

AM:
Not so much the land crabs. The blue crab, which is terrestrial, is still common, and there are even some times in the year when they are laying eggs that they flood the edge of the city. But the lobster, the *jaiba*, the black crab that is in fact from Caibarién, and which is the most famous in Cuba, because of how attractive and large it is. Perhaps it isn't so much the quantity, as the change that has taken place in its habitat, in the egg-laying zones, in its journey to find egg-laying zones and refuge, that they have been avoiding this zone.

Reptiles as well. You now hardly see iguanas. Domestic reptiles also have become scarce. So yes, there has been a notable impact on the fauna. Not so much in the vegetation, at least I haven't noticed much of an effect. But on the fauna, yes, it is noticeable.

Crab sculpture at the entrance to Caibarién (2019)
Photo: Wilder Llanes Márquez

PG:
The fishermen have to go out to sea. The bay is completely contaminated. There are some peripheral zones, on the edge of the insular platform where the open sea begins, where they tend to go to fish. There are many small keys were they used to go to fish, but not anymore.

Sponges, like corals, began to suffer deterioration in their proliferation due to the pollution of the sea, and the rise in temperatures. They are sensitive, like the corals, to all those adverse conditions that have been ruining some parts of the ecosystem.

As the whole world tries to wake up to the need for action to overcome such consequences of ecological damage, the attitude that it is always somebody else's problem or responsibility has to be overcome. This is as true in Cuba as it is anywhere. No doubt there will be a need to change our industrial and agricultural practices.

PG:
For me, the production of rum and tobacco in Cuba are amongst the most criminal – in my personal opinion. We are trying to save the earth or humanity, and we are poisoning human beings. Then we produce doctors so as to try to cure those people, but we previously poisoned them. If the state stopped assigning all these resources for those items that are profitable in financial terms, but aren't in health terms, I believe that the world would be grateful afterwards. Not immediately, because there are too many people who are dependent upon these pleasures; but the damage that is caused is much greater than the pleasure that they provide.

Even though there exists a ministry of ecology [the Ministry of Science, Technology and Environment, CITMA] that monitors and has struggled to try to stop the pollution, there is something that puts a brake on the attempt to decontaminate: and that is the economic and financial infrastructure of the country.

RF:
I think that what always happens is that there is a kind of conflict and contradiction between the economy and ecology. And in the end, often the factory, the business, the owners, those responsible, or the state, don't pay for this.

A country like Cuba depends on sugar. Obviously, first the companies, the businesses, then afterwards the state, have to maintain the sector alive, in order to obtain a source of income for the country.

But ultimately, it will come down to every one of us playing our part in being aware of what we have done, and are doing, to our environment – and finding new, improved ways of living.

MN:
Really it has to be said that the population in almost all the municipalities of the country does not perceive climate change at a local level. Perhaps they can tell you that it is a manifestation of climate change, because they have been taught about the melting of the ice caps, the disappearance of the glaciers. But its local manifestation, in that sense, I believe has to be worked on much more. Because the population isn't capable of perceiving, for example, that the minimum temperature has increased by 1.9°. They know it was hot at night, but they don't know what has really happened with the minimum temperatures in the locality. I think that it is up to us to tell them. There is a project on the local radio station to reflect on this. Modest studies have been made, and are sensitising the local population – not just with regards to the climate, but with everything related to the environment. It is necessary.

AM:
The only cause of this is social indiscipline. The lack of consciousness. The lack of love for nature and the environment. People who don't feel, and who don't see the danger of what they are doing with the contamination that they are creating. On the part of the population, there is a lot of social indiscipline. A genearlised lack of love and interest for taking care of the ecosystem, taking care of nature.

Also there has been damage caused because of the economic and social activity of the state. The River Guaní is totally polluted because of an alcohol distillery in one of the sugar centrals of the municipality. And there has been a lot of pollution of the coast, produced by the tipping of all kinds of waste from the hospital – because the plant that processed all this waste stopped working. It hasn't been started up again.

And all that waste, with toxic substances, is ending up in the sea, in an area near to the beach. Which must lead to damages. It must be causing problems, and at some point will have public health repercussions – if not now, then later.

And well, I think there already is something. Because, for example, we are suffering a dengue epidemic in the municipality, which even in 1981, when there was the great national epidemic, there wasn't such an impact here as there is now. And this all has to do with the lack of attention by the official state bodies, and the lack of internal discipline by the population for taking care of nature, of the environment. There is a lack of concern, a lot of indifference.

Thankfully, action is being taken. In March 2020, the Cuban government announced a general urban plan for Caibarién. This includes a revitalisation of the coastal areas, with a particular focus on mitigating the rising sea level, waves and other natural causes of coastal erosion that are impacting on the town. As well as seeking to improve water and energy provision in the area, measures are being taken to combat pollution, with the planned construction of two waste-processing plants (one for the fishing industry, and the other for the tannery). As the provincial director of the Institute for Physical Planning (*Instituto de Planificación Física*, IPF) commented:

> "The actions, in this case, have been directed towards evaluating the impacts associated with the inadequate management of waste liquids and the state of the prioritised ecosystems, incorporating into the programmes, plans, projects and current actions the informing about, promoting and acting in response to the identified environmental problems."

It remains to be seen how effectively these plans will be put into effect.

6 The Impact of Tourism

Tourism has a double impact: social and natural.

Abel Arnaldo González López

Caibarién is known by many today as being the town at the entry point to the chain of northern keys that have become popular tourist destinations, with holiday complexes catering mainly for foreign visitors seeking sun and sand in what they imagine to be pristine conditions. But locals remember a time when it was they who were able to enjoy them; and now there is increasing concern about the ecological, and social, impact that this development of tourism is having.

> *AAG:*
> I got to know Caibarién's keys when I was a boy. Back when the factory workers were rewarded with trips paid for by the state, they would take us there, which is how I knew Cayo Santa María, Cayo Ensenachos, when they were still unspoiled.

The keys remained relatively untouched because they were impossible to reach other than by boat. This gave them the feeling of being havens, filled with natural beauty, unique in their way, and worthy of preservation and protection. There was also a considerable feeling of local pride in them.

AM:
There is a species of snail. A type of liguus, called 'santamareare', which is unique to Cuba. We have them here in Cayo Santa María. There are abundant colonies, and it is a species that is symbolic of our municipality. We even have a festival of radio and television artists that is called Santamareare, in homage to that national snail, here in Caibarién.

AAG:
When there were underwater hunting competitions, my godfather would take us to the pontoon, to San Pascual, and the ship that was anchored there. That was where they carried out the sporting events of the national underwater hunting competition, over the course of fifteen or twenty days, at night and also during the day. We went to Cayo Fragoso, Cayo Francés. I didn't take part in the competition, but rather in the marine surroundings. I knew those keys.

Cayo Ensenachos, before the development of tourism
Photo courtesy of Pedro Manuel González Reinoso

***Liguus santamareare* shell**
Source: Emisora Provincial de Radio CMHW

PG:
I was fortunate to be able to go out on many of the boats in what was then called 'hydro-economy', because I had friends who were boat captains. And they invited me to discover all those zones that I hadn't seen – the whole of Buenavista Bay. And I saw how muddy its bed is. You could never find firm ground when you went diving. You could have the mud up to your chest, and you didn't touch ground.

But the idea arose that if a road could be constructed crossing the water to the keys, then they held an enormous amount of potential that could be tapped. As Cuba began looking to tourism as a possible solution to its economic problems, a project was developed to make this possible.

PG:
In the mid-1980s, a project was begun to construct a road to the keys. A causeway, a *pedraplén*. Before the economic collapse caused by the fall of the eastern bloc, the work had already begun to prepare for it. But it was during the Special Period that it became a priority for the government, because it was seen as a salvation in the midst of the misery.

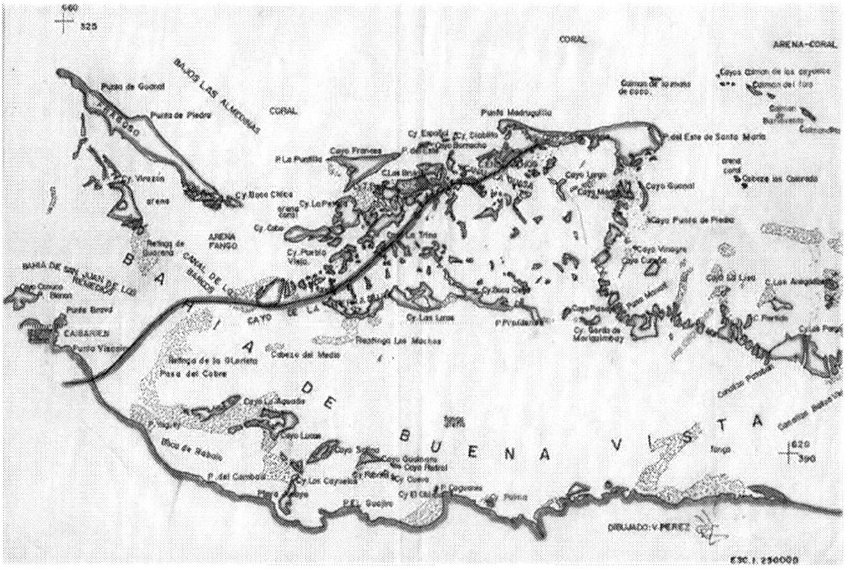

Map showing Caibarién, the keys and the causeway
Courtesy of Pedro Manuel González Reinoso

AAG:
In the 1990s, the country was in an economic crisis. Cuba had been left without allies and without countries to export to, without an import market. All friends had become enemies. The technology had changed. Without the importation of oil, the importation of primary resources, transport, agriculture and industry collapsed. It was a special situation. The economy collapsed by almost 40 percent in just four or five years. And naturally, tourism came to be seen as a great locomotive for pulling the economy. It freed up agriculture, construction and the entry of hard currency into the country.

Before the 1959 revolution, there was a substantial level of international tourism to Cuba. But this all but disappeared with the political change (with tourism widely being seen as a cause of many of the vices that were felt to be out of control in the country), and the economic embargo imposed by the US.

RF:
Before the revolution, Cuba used to receive 400,000 visitors a year, above all in Havana. A high-value tourism, coming mainly from the United States. In 1960, though, I think that Cuba received less than 500 tourists. And from then, until the 1980s, mass tourism doesn't restart. There was a residual tourism. Tourism from the socialist countries who came to Cuba. National tourism, which increased a lot during those years. There was an idea that national tourists should get to know these territories, outside of the city, to enable a better integration between the countryside and the city, and that Cubans might get to know more cut-off places, such as Ciénaga de Zapata, or the area of Pinar del Río, or areas in Oriente, where this kind of tourism was also developed, often connected with heritage.

I think there is also something that was postive in the long term for Cuba. From the 1960s, Cuba abandoned mass international tourism as a priority. So there wasn't that big boom of mass tourism that began in the 1960s, in the 1970s and 80s, which was based on large infrastructures. So Cuba, when it renounced that kind of tourism, had that kind of large infrastructure, but also had smaller scale tourism, that was more respectful of the environment, more integrated with the ecosystem, like the mangrove zones. More integrated with the mountain ecosystem. And I believe that this was an advantage.

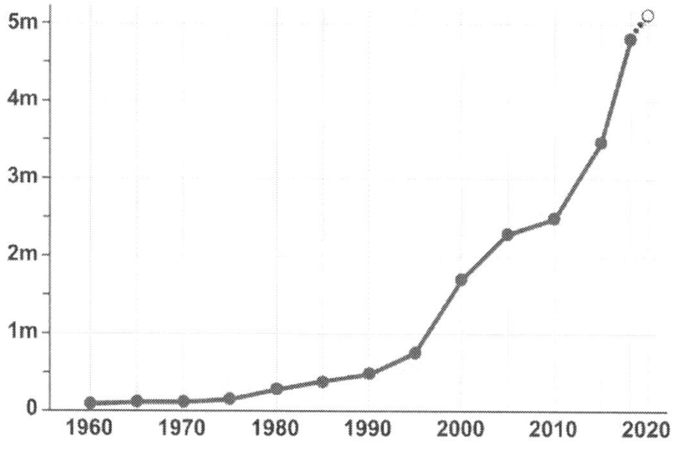

Numbers of foreign tourists arriving in Cuba (1960-2020)

Constructing the causeway to the keys (1990s)
Photo courtesy of Pedro Manuel González Reinoso

RF:
I think that up to a certain point, it was an advantage for Cuba that there was a pause in mass tourism, so as to be able to learn from the lessons of the damage that this kind of tourism caused in other places. These days there is an attempt not to construct on dunes, and there are plans to demolish those that were built on dunes. So I think these are very positive aspects. Which isn't to say that in Cuba there isn't the same environmental impact of mass tourism, or cruise tourism, but really there is a concern for trying to minimise as much as possible this environmental impact.

Tourism today is like the new frontier of the global economy in Cuba. It is what the neighbouring countries surrounding Cuba depend upon. So tourism has been becoming the principal sector of the economy, as sugar was in its time. Perhaps sugar is the best comparison. There has been a transfer from the sugar frontier to the tourism frontier.

As the country again looked to tourism as a source of revenue in the 1990s, when the sugar industry was suffering from low world prices and the country had lost the beneficial trade it had enjoyed with the Soviet Union and socialist bloc, the idea of constructing a causeway to the keys became very attractive. The plans were rushed through, as the country hurried to find a way to overcome the severe economic crisis it had been plunged into.

PG:
The work was carried out in a hurry. I was working in agriculture, in Dolores, and every day I passed where they were making the causeway. It worried me that the hill of Guajabana was losing half its structure, which was being thrown into the sea. But if they were doing it for a good purpose, then I supposed it was fine.

The causeway was one of the longest in Cuba. It has the same length as the distance from Caibarién to the provincial capital, Santa Clara. It was built in two directions, until they met in the middle, in the shipping channel. From over there, they had a fleet of lorries that were initially taken across on barges, that tipped rocks into the sea. Because it was easier to join the keys, because of their closeness, than to join the north of Villa Clara to the keys. The hard job was from here to there. There also weren't enough quarries to complete the job, so they had to dig out earth from many places.

Loma Guajabana, showing damage (present day)
Photo: Eliecer Turó González

AAG:
There were more bridges than kilometres, and it even won the Puente de Alcántara Prize, given by Spain.

PG:
An international prize that is given to the most important constructions, the largest that have been made on the planet. There is a plaque there that commemorates the prize, which consisted in a large amount of money. I imagine they did a lot of promotion to make the award possible. They were very interested in securing the money, so as to help save the causeway in the future.

Inevitably, such a substantial engineering project, cutting across Buenavista Bay and joining the mainland to the islands, was likely to have an environmental impact.

PG:
What intrigued me was how they were going to make the causeway with sufficient quality that it would guarantee that the area wasn't affected ecologically. Constructing an artificial causeway over the sea has to have consequences. It isn't the same as constructing a road on columns. But here there wasn't the money to do that.

AAG:
At one time, when we were young, we dreamed of having a road like that. But it had a natural impact. That area is a National Biosphere Reserve, part of the Buenavista reserve, which is made up of a coastal zone in Villa Clara and the north of Sancti Spíritus, and the north of Ciego de Avila, and the corresponding maritime zone. With a high degree of endemism of flora and fauna.

When I heard that they were going to make the causeway, I said that it was going to have an impact on the biosphere. They tried to reduce this, having had the experience of the Bay of Los Perros, and the causeway that was built between the north of Ciego de Avila and Cayo Coco. Here they built some 48 km of road and 49 bridges.

AM:
The construction of the Caibarién-Cayo Santa María causeway added an artificial obstacle. Although all its drainage channels were well studied, nevertheless it has to have had an impact, being an anthropic agent, in the ecological balance of many species. In their habitat and in their movements to lay eggs, to reproduce. Yes, there has been an effect.

PG:
Fortunately, the causeway included strategic bridges to let the currents through.

AAG:
They foresaw that having the bridges would allow the marine currents to flow, and so the impact was less.

PG:
Even so, the migration of animals changed. The ecosystem changed. The flora changed.

Cayo Santa María tourist complex (2019)
Photo: Gonzalo Vidal

Cayo Santa María beach (2019)
Photo: Gonzalo Vidal

AM:
The causeway has affected the habitat of marine species. The flora must also have been affected, because there are many shorelines of the keys that the causeway passes by, where the equilibrium was broken. All those animal and plant species suffered damage. They had to leave to find new places of refuge.

PG:
The causeway began to suffer damage to its bridges. What's sad is that the materials that were used were not of the best quality, and they immediately showed signs of deterioration. The bridges began to suffer from salinisation caused by the sea, from the winds, from the tide, from climate change, from everything. And it became necessary to carry out urgent repairs. True, a bridge has never completely collapsed. But they have been gradually falling to pieces. And it was necessary to restructure them. This has brought additional ecological damage. Because they have had to throw more materials into the sea, and close off the current. Although this was done in a temporary way, these channels used to be open, but had to be closed in order to repair the structures. And some of them were quite large.

If the causeway had an environmental impact, the development of tourism on the keys certainly has.

AM:
There was an impact, from the construction of hotels. That broke the ecological balance of the keys. It has provoked the emigration of species. The destruction or damage to many plant species.

AAG:
I would have liked the keys to have had a low-impact tourism. Few installations, very expensive so as to attract millionaires. Because that would have led to a more responsible exploitation of the keys. But instead they bet on mass tourism. With the economic blockade, Cuba was never going to get a tourism of millionaires. Impossible. And with the urgent necessity that the country had to obtain hard currency, and to create employment and recover the economy, I can understand that it was necessary to promote a massification of tourism. Which is what occurred. Personally, I don't like it. But I understand the need that the country had at that moment. And they built many hotels, and they are still building.

PG:
Hundreds of keys that were natural refuges for fishermen when there was bad weather, when there were sea swells. And now they can't go there, because it is a zone that is completely dedicated to tourism. And after they constructed the causeway, there were even more restrictions.

Fishing has been amongst the heaviest hit. They say that the level of fishes is still there, but there are zones that have been declared exclusive for tourism. For example, the tourists can pay to go out on a catamaran to fish. It is an adventure. Those zones have stopped being fishing zones, because they are now reserved exclusively for tourism.

AAG:
When you take flowers and plants to decorate the hotels, that has an impact on autochthonous plant life. The vegetation on those islands – which are rocky keys, or coral keys, or sandy keys – is distinctive. What there is most of is coastal swamp vegetation, and plants on sandy land, not to mention the aquatic plant life, which is very abundant.

AAG:
If plants are brought in for decoration, then there is an anthropic modification. You get ornamental plants that are typical of cities. And that is naturally going to have an impact. I still go to the keys, and I see both the autochthonous fauna and what has been introduced. And naturally, however much you try to mitigate the impact, it will always be seen.

PG:
The wells that supplied Caibarién with water were very large, and they were deviated to supply the keys. That's when the town began to be supplied by smaller wells, and the salinisation of the water increased. Because too much was being taken out. And when you take out all the water that is left, the water table is refilled with whatever is nearby. And what you have nearby is the sea, which is why the water is salty. The water near to the coasts is very salty.

But for all the fears about what the environmental cost might be, there was also hope in the local population of Caibarién that their proximity to the new tourist developments would have a positive impact on the town's economy. This, however, turned out not to be the case.

PG:
When they at last opened the causeway, and they began to construct the first hotels, the people fervently hoped that Caibarién was going to become the Cárdenas of Villa Clara. The city of Cárdenas has been very prosperous, because of the proximity of Varadero. But that never occurred here.

AAG:
It is a problem of identity. Caibarién is the closest place. It ought to be the logical place for the tourist who is tired of the beach to have contact with the other Cuba. The Cuba that is more than hotels. But you don't feel that contact that Caibarién ought to have benefitted from. I believe that the local authorities, in general, either couldn't or didn't want to encourage this contact.

I remember that they made a town in the midst of the hotels. A town that was an appendix to the hotels. The same construction, the same format, the same services, but which had to be paid for. And afterwards they made four more. Why didn't they put that investment into Caibarién?

AAG:
More was done in Remedios, which is the heritage city. Remedios has been able to regrow its laurels with tourism. But not Caibarién. Over the last 27 years I have travelled around the country. I have seen it collapse and I have seen it rise out of the economic crisis. Why is it that those other towns have grown and left the crisis behind, but I have not seen that in Caibarién? In Caibarién what I have seen is that it is moving backwards, always backwards.

PG:
This city never saw the fruits of all that construction. Lamentably. The money that the keys and the causeway brought, was destined for other purposes, about which the local administration had no say.

Resort hotel rooms on Cayo Santa María (2019)
Photo: Gonzalo Vidal

Restored church in Remedios (2016)
Photo: Wilder Llanes Méndez

PG:
The local lament is that we only got what the users of those resources decided to grant us. And because of this, we are in such a precarious situation.

AAG:
It bothers me when I hear the propaganda about tourism in Caibarién, and I see that they talk about the 'northern keys of Villa Clara'. That bothers me. These were always the northern keys of Caibarién, because who was it who were concerned for those keys? It was the fishermen and the charcoal burners of Caibarién. It was always Caibarién that paid attention to the keys. I think it is a problem of identity that is being lost. Those hotels come, and there are references to Santiago de Cuba, Trinidad, Havana. But why don't they refer to Caibarién? Or maybe even Remedios, which is nearby. Why not?

Despite their proximity, it proved to be rather difficult for the inhabitants of Caibarién even to obtain employment in the new hotels.

AAG:
Caibarién doesn't have a school for training tourism workers, which it should have because we are close.

PG:
I began to have problems with the local government when I pointed out that it didn't make sense opening a tourism school in Santa Clara, when the workforce ought to be next to the hotels. There were people in Caibarién looking for work in tourism, but the provincial authorities gave priority to their own people to go to the preparatory schools. It was just for their own.

The directors of tourism, the employing companies like Gaviota, opened those spaces, and prioritised their families and their friends. Even though there was a local population that was economically unemployed, and eager to enter, but did not have what was required, because they gave priority to whoever they wanted.

AAG:
It's true that work opportunities have to be given to the whole province. But they have brought many workers from distant parts of Villa Clara. Workers who have to be brought in buses, with the consequent consumption of fuel. They could have privileged Caibarién much more.

PG:
There are sommeliers there who travel every day from Trinidad in transport that goes to collect them, because there is nobody here who can substitute them. They cross the entire province, and then 50 km along the causeway, and return – when they don't stay for a couple of days, which is difficult because they don't have living quarters for these people. At least, not unless there is a hurricane, when they house personnel there hermetically, so as to help with the reconstruction. But not when there's tourism.

This makes the transportation considerably more expensive, totalling thousands of kilometres every day, once you add it all together. It's 100 km to travel from Santa Clara to the keys, and the same going back. It's horrible, and these people are suffering physically from it.

AAG:
They built a new neighbourhood here. They are encouraging immigration into Caibarién from the rest of the province. New people are coming, but they don't have roots here. It is a desirable immigration in one sense, because they are professionals, selected workers. So it isn't like when Australia was filled with delinquents. But they don't have roots here. The future generations of descendants will have, but they don't now.

Unfortunately, Caibarién hasn't been alone in seeming not to benefit locally from the rise of tourism. Other communities around Cuba are feeling the disparities of advantage.

AVE:
In Artemisa I asked many young people from the former sugar town if they had been able to find employment in tourism, and they told me that this had been one of the promises that they were made. That since there was that source of work nearby, that was opening up with such strength, they were going to prioritise the local population. But unfortunately, it hasn't been that way. They have brought workers from other places, because of personal relationships or perhaps because of specific skills, to take the positions of responsibility. And very few have come from the locality.

In Matanzas, for example, there is a lot of immigration from the eastern provinces, possibly via the Isle of Pines, which was a trampoline to get to the western provinces. There was space, there was housing there, there were offers of work, and there were many people from the eastern provinces. Frequent cases of clandestine immigration. Young fathers of families who suddenly, in a relatively short period of time, prepared their journey, and came there in order to get to Varadero. These people occupied houses that had been left empty, or the spaces that had been offices that had closed.

In Caibarién, not only is it felt that there was a failure to give the local population a fair share of the new jobs that were being established, but also in other respects the local economy – which might have been well-placed to help service the tourist installations – was sidelined.

AAG:
The majority of the decorative plants have been brought to the hotels from Sancti Spíritus. Why not from Caibarién? I know that much of the land here isn't good, but there is very good agricultural land towards Dolores, and as far as I know no food is being grown there for those hotels, which have a lot of need. That could naturally increase the importance of the local economy, and of the private economy, there in Dolores, which falls under the administrative control of Caibarién.

With popular discontent about this situation simmering in Caibarién – with the local population not only now effectively excluded from enjoying the keys, but also not feeling they are receiving any of the benefits accruing from tourism – the authorities attempted to assuage local feelings by making some improvements to the town's facilities. However, this does not seem to have been as successful as was hoped.

PG:
Around the turn of the century, the local government suggested beautifying the local beach, because the citizens were unhappy that there were some keys that used to belong to them, which were now occupied by tourism, and now they couldn't go to them as ordinary citizens, because for a long time all access was forbidden. They couldn't go there. They were an exclusive ghetto for tourists and the military, who could access them with complete freedom. They, their families, etcetera. And the workers saw them going, and this is a regrettable difference that hurt them.

So, the local government proposed improving Caibarién's beach, with the support of the national government. And for what? The beach's existing structures were demolished. It had walls that divided it into segments – based on a very old study showing that with artificial sands on improvised beaches, the only way to stop the waves eroding the sand is the construction of containing walls. These walls were ripped out, because somebody decided that these walls were prehistoric, from the first years of the twentieth century, which is when the beach was divided: military beach, black beach (which was the beach of the poor), the Yacht Club, and all that.

Caibarién beach, today (2019)
Photos: Gonzalo Vidal

PG:
The beach was devastated and converted into what it is now: which is nothing. It is a lagoon where every year, as a consequence of that erroneous decision, sand is laid down, and the season hasn't even finished and the sand has already gone, because there aren't any containing walls.

I heard someone suggest that it is necessary to remake the beach walls, so that our people can enjoy a small piece of summer, a place to bathe in. Because this used to be a much-visited beach. The whole province came here. There were long-established campsites. Now practically all those places have disappeared, and the beach now has no comforts. On the contrary. It is rank.

Nevertheless, in one respect there does seem to have been a local success story related to tourism. The closing of the town's only remaining sugar factory, the Reforma, saw the loss of many local jobs – and one of the remaining symbols of the town's former economic strength. However, this has since been repurposed as a museum.

MP:
The sugar mill that the museum is located in dates from 1891, and was brought to a stop in 1999. This paralysation occurred due to the drop in the international price of sugar, making it unprofitable for the country to maintain many of these sugar factories working. The socialist camp, and the Soviet Union, also collapsed, and it was no longer profitable for Cuba because we couldn't sell all the sugar, or have so many sugar factories in such a situation. So the Government decided to bring to a halt several sugar factories, and convert them into other social uses. This one was converted into a museum. Here we show to the younger generations, and any visitors, the history of sugar production. The museum opened in 2002.

OZ:
I don't know what led to the decision. Evidently it must have been influenced by the fact that it was in a zone with tourist possibilities. The intention was to try to preserve a sugar mill museum in every province. In this case, the Reforma was chosen as being the mill in Villa Clara most favourable for becoming a museum.

Sugar museum, Caibarién (2019)
Photo: Gonzalo Vidal

OZ:
In the end, only four provinces got their sugar museums. These were Matanzas, Villa Clara, Sancti Spíritus (in the Valley of the Sugar Mills, *Valle de los Ingenios*, in Trinidad), and Ciego de Avila. Which are all central provinces. As you will realise, the four museums are in touristic zones. The Reforma is close to Cayo Santa María, the Patria is in the Morón zone, in the area where the tourists enter and leave for Cayo Guillermo and Cayo Coco. That of Trinidad, obviously it's in a very touristic area, with its *Valle de los Ingenios*. And that of Matanzas is at the entrance to Varadero.

MP:
We have a theme park with steam engines: thirty-eight steam locomotives. We show how the sugar industry developed, from the introduction of sugarcane into our country. It originally came from New Guinea, and was introduced on the second voyage of Christopher Columbus to the Canary Islands, and then what is now the Dominican Republic. And Diego Velázquez introduced it into Cuba between 1511 and 1524.

The factory here was originally the Central Reforma (then later the Marcelo Salado). All the machinery here is original. When the factory ceased production in 1999, all the original pieces were kept here, from which the sugar used to be produced. Over the course of the years, in our country the sugar industry was like the old cars – the Chevrolet or Mercedes, that is the old cars you still see around – which are continually repaired. That's what happens with the old cars. That's what happens with the sugar machinery. These machines were constantly repaired. On occasions pieces were replaced with those that were manufactured here, but always onto the same base.

This sugar factory always had an industrial chromatics. The pieces are identified by different colours. The moving parts are coloured green. The water is signified by the colour blue. The steam with grey. So the meaning of each part is visible. As a museum we try to maintain this chromatism.

The sugar museum, along with the proximity of the keys, and Caibarién's own coast (albeit somewhat delapidated) and the town's idiosyncratic

Sugar museum interior, Caibarién (2019)
Photo: Gonzalo Vidal

character and heritage does bring some visitors in. The town is certainly full of houses attempting to make business as hostals, as the plethora of signs to be seen in the street atest. However, much of this is more out of optimism that Caibarién will eventually benefit from its location, rather than a sign of flourishing trade.

In general, the challenge facing Cuba – like many other places – is how the undoubted potential economic benefits of tourism can be harnessed in a way that is sustainable: both ecologically and socially.

RF:
When they speak about tourism these days in the Caribbean, many people identify it with the plantation era. It's as though it had been inherited from colonialism, with the same dependent relationship between poor countries and rich countries. And if not the only alternative, it is the principal alternative that has been left to many Caribbean countries, which depend increasingly on these flows of tourists.

Contrary to what you might think, that this is an industry without chimneys, in reality tourism has an enormous environmental cost, because of the flow of materials and energy for the journeys. Bringing people to the Caribbean costs a lot. It requires a lot of energy. And this is interesting, because originally the Caribbean exported calories. Now we have to think how many calories are needed to bring all this tourism infrastructure. The people who take part, who come to enjoy the Caribbean sun and beaches. Often the increase in food imports to sustain this. The demand for water. So really, contrary to the image of an industry without chimneys, there is a high demand for energy and materials to sustain this industry. Starting with the transatlantic flights. The large cruise ships. And this makes the Caribbean economy more vulnerable and more dependent.

There have been studies about tourism, that suggest that a large part of the profits remains outside the host countries. And basically in the Caribbean (which is one of the areas with the highest penetration of the international tourist industry), a large part of the profit remains in the countries of origin, in the former metropoles. That's why many people, many scholars have made this connection between the plantation and tourism, seeing it as a new expression of this plantation economy.

Guest house signs in Caibarién (2019) (this page and next)

Photos: Gonzalo Vidal

HOSTAL
Restaurante
EL COLISEO
ESTRELLA
HOSTA
RENT ROOMS
HOSTAL
VISTA AL MAR
HOSTAL
YAYO
El pescador
HOSTAL
ROOM FOR RENT
HOSTAL
Hostal
HOSTAL
EL MARINO
Sr. Osmany Dominguez
HOSTAL
20 MILLAS
SANTA MARIA
500m
RENT ROOMS
HOSTAL
PARE

RF:
Now we should be also thinking what other alternatives there might be in this globalised world, for a region that is so vulnerable to tourism. I believe that the Cuban model seeks to keep the highest possible percentage of the profits in the country, which is why they have a model of mixed companies – combining state and foreign businesses, thereby guaranteeing a certain percentage of the profits remain in the country.

Obviously, it is a debate. And I believe that the people who are working in this – both in government and in tourism – like the organisations and the scientific institutions, are very conscious of this reality. And we need to seek a balance.

There is a certain advantage in that Cuba has escaped, for almost thirty years, mass tourism, which has permitted the country to learn other lessons. But obviously it isn't free of those environmental impacts, especially in this tourism boom in Cuba. And there is a need to try to prevent there being an even greater impact in the future.

AF:
I think that if an intelligent policy can be developed, really prioritising local development, which connects these small, traditional towns with a very old culture related to the sea, with craft fishing and the like – it might be possible for these to become tourist attractions for the area, in the development of its tourism.

What is happening is that the tourism that is now developing in Cuba tends to either be city tourism, or sun-and-beach tourism. Like in Varadero, like in the area of the North Villa Clara keys. And it is a very closed tourism. They see it as a closed tourism, package tourism, which doesn't offer those kinds of possibilities. I think that all these small coastal towns could have an economic reactivation if public policy can be connected a little more dynamically to the development of tourism.

But while there has been no shortage of tourism aimed at exploiting the obvious advantages of sun, sea and sand, Cuba has also seen the gradual development of a different kind of tourism. One that seeks to be in greater harmony with the environment and the community.

RF:

The 1990s saw a big advance for all kinds of tourism in Cuba: mass tourism, tourism of sun and beach, and also a kind of tourism more directed inland. More connected to natural values, and historic values as well. A lot of work has gone into restoring archaeological sites. I think that in this Cuba has a lot of potential, using such places that were abandoned by the agricultural frontier, in order to show as well what the country was historically, and how it has been transformed.

There are many examples of ecotourism. Ecotourism which was promoted particularly after the 1960s. Two of the most emblematic places are Las Terrazas and the Ciénaga de Zapata.

Las Terrazas started as a reforestation project but also already potentially connected to ecotourism – although it was after the 1980s that really there was a big rise, a much greater push towards ecotourism, and above all after the 1990s.

Since the 1960s, the Ciénaga de Zapata has had an emphasis on combining other projects that then existed, like the drainage project in certain zones for the production of rice, along with these ecotourism projects.

Cuban crocodile, Ciénaga de Zapata (2008)
Photo: Gonzalo Vidal

Guamá ecotourism village, Ciénaga de Zapata (2008)
Photo: Gonzalo Vidal

In Guamá, for example. I had a student who worked on the theme of the Taino village, and Guamá as an ecotourism project, and who demonstrates how there was a transformation from one kind of tourism that existed above all until the 1950s (although already in the 1950s they were beginning to evaluate this other kind of project that was more in contact with nature). Some of these projects in the Ciénaga de Zapata began to appear before, but really materialised after the 1960s. They established a crocodile breeding station as well. And nowadays one of the fundamental activities in the Ciénaga de Zapata is ecotourism.

Pinar del Río is one of the principal provinces for ecotourism. Viñales, for example, which was a project that began before the revolution, and in recent years has been on the rise, above all connected to agritourism and ecotourism. I think that those two develop together.

Viñales valley, Pinar del Río, Cuba (2013)
Photo: Gonzalo Vidal

RF:
In 1968, a reforestation project was begun in the Sierra del Rosario, along with the production of coffee. And that's when they began the project of Las Terrazas. A community was constructed, so that this community could bring together all the peasants who were living in the area in very poor conditions. They were brought together in the community to give them electricity, drinking water, better housing, and they built something along the lines of what today might be called an 'ecological' or 'sustainable' community, though perhaps at that time this wasn't the term. But there was already a concern for this relationship with the environment. This community was devoted primarily to the reforestation of all this territory. There were plans for large-scale reforestation, using a system of terraces that were constructed, and for this reason the community was given the name Las Terrazas.

From the start they included components for tourism. Ecological tourism we might call this today, which began to develop much more after the 1990s, but this already existed as well.

In 1983, thanks to the success of all these reforestation plans throughout this territory, the area of Sierra del Rosario was granted by UNESCO the status of being a biosphere reserve. It was the first in Cuba to be named a biosphere reserve. And much of this was the result of a process of restoration of this whole landscape after 1968, but above all after 1971, which is when the community was formally created.

There was a lot of involvement here by the Academy of Sciences, along with Osmany Cienfuegos, who was the architect who created this project along with a group of scientists who came to carry out several studies, from the point of view of the natural sciences, from the point of view of the social sciences, of this whole community that lived around what is now the community of Las Terrazas.

It is to be hoped that such projects may offer a path towards a more sustainable approach to the Cuba's future

Las Terrazas community and ecotourism centre, Sierra del Rosario (2019)
Photo: Gonzalo Vidal

7 Sustainable Futures

I am optimistic. We are going to reach the point when either we come to an agreement with nature, or we come to an agreement – because there is no other way out. There is only one planet. The fertile land is being exhausted, and in the end we are going to say 'this is bad'. We are going to end up respecting each other, and find a solution.

Manuel Iturralde-Vinent

The project that resulted in the making of the documentary *Cuba: Living Between Hurricanes* – and upon which this book has been based – started out with the intention of looking at the past, present and future of a coastal community in Cuba through the lens of hurricanes, and the impact that they have. However, important and spectacular in their destructive potential though these storms are, what became clear was that the real question is much bigger than how to cope with these meteorological events when they arrive. It is not only about surviving hurricanes, or even living with hurricanes. What is key is how we live between them. Whether communities can find ways through which their vulnerability can be minimised, and long-term future secured, regardless of what nature might throw at them. As elsewhere in the world, the on-going, and intensifying, effects of climate change and environmental degradation are making the search for a sustainable future ever more pressing.

Since the arrival of the Spanish in the sixteenth century, possibly the most noticeable environmental change that has affected Cuba has been its radical deforestation. It has been claimed that there was a time when it would have been possible to walk from one end of the island to the other always under the shadow of the trees. Those days have long gone, much of this the result of the intensive cultivation of sugarcane using methods that favoured clearing land, exhausting the soil, and then moving on to exploit new terrain. Nevertheless, slowly awareness has grown in Cuba for the need to take measures to restrict the damage that was being caused.

RF:
In 1926 for the first time a decree was established prohibiting the growing of sugarcane on forested highlands. Up until then, above all since 1815 when Spain permitted private individuals to cut down the forests, the deforestation accelerated with the expansion of the sugar frontier. Between 1815 and 1926 there was practically no restriction, on private land (which accounted for the largest part of the island), to what the owners could do with these forests. And this obviously contributed to the rise of the sugar industry.

After 1926, there were progressively more restrictions on the use of forested lands in the production of sugarcane, or other kinds of crops. But the reality is that by then there practically weren't any primary forests left on flat land.

Although there were those who were expressing concerns in the late-nineteenth and early-twentieth centuries about the ecological state of the island, and the detrimental impact that sugar cultivation in particular was having, it was not until relatively recently that serious attempts were made to change the dominant culture of indiscriminate environmental exploitation.

AF:
Really here in Cuba there have been different moments in the development of the consciousness of citizens in relation to the environment and its problems. I would say that towards the end of the 1980s, several social scientists indicated the need for local policies geared to local sustainable development.

Nevertheless, for a long period this was not taken sufficiently into account. Public policy opened up above all after the Rio Summit, in which Fidel gave an incredible speech about the need for a global consciousness concerning the environment. It marked one of the defining moments in national politics with respect to sustainable development.

This speech by Fidel Castro at the 1992 Earth Summit in Rio de Janeiro has since been seen as marking a political turning point in the Cuban state's recognition of the importance of such questions – even if Fidel's argument was that the fault for the environmental crisis lay primarily with wealthy capitalist countries:

> An important biological species – humankind – is at risk of disappearing due to the rapid and progressive elimination of its natural habitat. We are becoming aware of this problem when it is almost too late to prevent it... The forests are disappearing. The deserts are expanding. Billions of tons of fertile soil are washed every year into the sea. Numerous species are becoming extinct. Population pressures and poverty lead to desperate efforts to survive, even at the expense of nature... Unequal trade, protectionism and foreign debt assault the ecological balance and promote the destruction of

Fidel Castro, speaking at the Rio Earth Summit (1992)

> the environment. If we want to save humanity from this self-destruction, wealth and available technologies must be distributed better throughout the planet. Less luxury and less waste in a few countries would mean less poverty and hunger in much of the world.

Rousing though Fidel's speech undoubtedly was – and shocking that thirty years later his words still ring just as true – if change is to come, it must start at home – regardless of the political system or ruling ideology. It is all very well pointing the finger of blame, but practical measures also need to be undertaken where we ourselves live, attempting to make our own communities ecologically and socially sustainable. In Cuba, certainly there were political measures taken that seemed to be on the right tracks.

> *AF:*
> In 1992, coinciding with the Rio Summit, the Ministry of Science, Technology and the Environment (CITMA) was formed out of the Academy of Sciences, and one of its priorities – which continues now – is precisely the achievement of national sustainable development. Nevertheless, so long as macroeconomic policies are not connected to local development, there is always going to be something missing in the implementation of public policies in relation to the citizenry.

It has too often felt in Cuba, as indeed elsewhere around the world, that high sounding discourse has not transposed into effective action where it is really needed.

> *AF:*
> They subordinated the local sphere to the general politics of the nation.
>
> *OZ:*
> Fidel Castro considered that land that could be used for the production of human food should not be given to the production of biofuel. So former cane land was supposed to be given to other crops or to pasture. It was going to be dedicated to the development of food production. However, in practice most of this land became invaded by sicklebush (*marabú*).

Nevertheless, there are those who have seen opportunity in the apparent ecological crisis, and are looking for effective solutions.

AM:
The lands taken over by sicklebush are effectively deserted, because it's impossible to penetrate them due to the thorns that they have. In order to alleviate the damage, to clean up what was done wrong, the sicklebush is being used a lot for charcoal, which is valued internationally. They are exporting hundreds of tons. Thousands of tons of charcoal made from sicklebush. At least it is being given an economic use now.

Since 2019, attempts are also being made to use the abundant sicklebush to generate electricity in Cuba, thereby helping to overcome the power crisis in the country, and reduce the reliance on oil.

Biomass energy plant being transported, Cuba (2019)
Photo: Pedro Manuel González Reinoso

But in Caibarién, little is yet being done to adopt new practices.

PG:
Ecological and organic agriculture is practically unheard of here [in Caibarién]. There are some experiments in some areas, where they are doing things. There are smallholdings where they are using animal waste, for example of cows, to help production. The bagasse of the cane is used for energy. There are some programmes. The use of wind power to generate electricity. There are some transformations that have gradually taken place in the country, but they are still small.

Nevertheless, the economic crisis of the 1990s, the so-called 'Special Period', of necessity led Cuba to seek out sustainable agricultural methods that would enable the country to feed itself in conditions of severe shortages in fuel, fertilisers, and pretty much everything else.

Smallholding near Caibarién (2008)
Photo: Pedro Manuel González Reinoso

RF:
Ecological agriculture emerged in Cuba, above all organic agriculture, during the Special Period, in order to change the model of a conventional industrialised agriculture, towards a model of agriculture that would be more sustainable, less dependent upon the large-scale use of resources, and agro-chemicals.

While initially this occurred in a piecemeal way, more recently there have been some rather more concerted efforts to develop new, sustainable approaches to agriculture – combining the latest scientific advances with a recovery of traditional skills. These projects, often the result of individual initiative, are aimed both at proving the economic and ecological viability of such approaches, and serving as pilots in the hope that the methods they are developing may eventually be more generally applied across the island.

One particularly prominent example of this, which has received a lot of international attention, is Finca Marta, just fifteen miles south-west of Havana.

FF:
Finca Marta is an agro-ecological project founded in 2011, and dedicated to the memory of our mother. She was a biologist, who focused on the development of ecological agriculture in Cuba and was the principal inspiration for this project. In my academic work, alongside her, we were researching ecological agriculture, the integration of cattle and crop growing, multifunctional systems and agricultural diversity. We have tried to put into practice all these technical concepts and theories, in a concrete setting from a social and an economic point of view. Social in that it fits into the local rural dynamic; and it has to be economically sustainable.

The nearby sugar central closed around 2002, and this whole area was somewhat abandoned. The cattle began to disperse the sicklebush, which in a few years had completely covered the area. With land being leased to those who wanted to work it, there were a few smallholdings that were cleared. But the majority of the zone had been invaded by sicklebush. We had to clear the whole of the land, and we have to continue clearing because there are still many seeds left in the soil, and the sicklebush resprouts from its roots. If you don't keep clearing, then in a few months it's grown high again.

Finca Marta, Caimito, Cuba (2019)
Photo: Gonzalo Vidal

FF:
We were told that the land was only good for cattle. Nevertheless, I was convinced that it could produce other things. We began with apiculture, and started having bees. After six years, we now have around a hundred hives, and we produce a lot of honey. Last year we had around ten tons of honey. We also cultivate vegetables. We knew that by improving the soil, regenerating the soil, adding organic material, then we could produce vegetables, which don't need such deep soil. And we gradually transformed the area to enable the production of vegetables. Vegetables have been our principal income, and have maintained an average of fifteen families, earning money and sustaining themselves from this. The families that work here.

Our project focused on achieving the capacity to generate an income, to generate well-being, and generate a continuity to the process. If there isn't money, if there isn't income that allows investing in sustaining the livelihood of the rural population, to be able to pay an acceptable level of salary, to be able to invest to cover the operative costs (because everyday there are costs that have to be covered), then the system wouldn't be able to replicate itself.

This has been a critique for ecological agriculture, agroecology, seen as a subsistence system. But we are not talking about a subsistence system, we are talking about a system that can be replicated, and which can be expanded, so as to have an ever greater economic and social impact. That is one of the fundamental challenges facing agroecology and ecological agriculture, because while you preserve the environment, you are spending time, work and money. And there needs to be an efficient production system, economically viable, that sustains this.

If you can count on the support of the government, if you can count on outside financial support, perfect. But if not, then it has to be generated by the system itself.

We have had a fundamental impact on the volume of production, in the diversity of production, in the quality of the product that we send to the restaurants, and stability during the whole year. In the last two years we have been working for the local market, and we succeeded in establishing three new farms in other areas of the town of Caimito; and we have been distributing to around twenty social institutions. Schools, nurseries, old people's homes.

Finca Marta, Caimito, Cuba (2019)
Photo: Gonzalo Vidal

FF:
We produce milk, meat, cheese, for our own consumption. But also for visitors, because we provide agritourism. We receive agritourism groups, that come once or twice a week. Although it is an important source of income, it is more important for us to be concentrating on improving the agricultural system – and so we see agritourism as a complementary activity. This generates some income at certain moments, but which interlocks with the improvement and protection of the environment, and the agricultural production system.

The idea is to achieve energy sustainability of the system. Perhaps before the end of 2019, we will already have sufficient generation and capture of energy in order to maintain the whole demand of the system. Not just the demand for the house, for everything that has to do with domestic consumption, but also for the whole productive system. That is, the pumping of water, the cutting of forage, everything.

We have four fundamental pillars in our daily work. One is agricultural production and the environment: that is, to produce food in harmony with the environment, caring for the environment, and establishing ecological systems of production. Second, education and research. We promote various educational and research systems, which enable an understanding of how the ecosystem works; and enables its replication. A third pillar is the development of the market system, the development of the system of commercialisation to different market sectors. And the fourth pillar is the agritourism. And with the agritourism we also connect with the educational system.

Our objective, now that we have arrived at a level of organisation, a technological level, a level of social and economic coherence, the feasibility of the system that we have been able to prove – we are proposing to the local government the expansion into becoming a sustainable agricultural community. That means other farmers establishing themselves in the zone, in order to establish a communal dynamic, which will permit having a greater impact from the point of view of the four pillars that we have: agricultural production and the environment; education and research; commercialisation; and agritourism systems that connect with the wider territory, and not just with a single farm.

It is to be hoped that practical examples like Finca Marta may offer a

***Working in Finca Marta* (2019)**
Image taken from film *Cuba: Living Between Hurricanes*

direction in which agriculture may develop in the future – not only in Cuba, but globally. Seeking ways that work with the environment, not against it; and which can provide a means for supporting local communities in sustainable ways.

> *FF:*
> I think that in any part of the world, in any part of Cuba, agriculture is possible. There are more or less resources of one kind or another. There are places, for example, of conventional agriculture in the south of Havana, that have the best lands in Cuba, but the most unproductive systems. It depends on how the system is connected to the natural resources. It depends on how they have been integrated.

In many ways, Cuba is seeking to lead the way in adapting to the need for more sustainable and resilient approaches. Katherine Angier, in reporting to the US-based Environmental Defense Fund in March 2020, looked at the lessons that can be learned from what the island has been doing:

> Cuba is preparing its agricultural sector for a future with unpredictable weather, severe storms and rising seas. The plan includes government programs aimed at building resilient farms through the adoption of

conservation practices that increase water-use efficiency, improved drought resilience and deliver some other unexpected benefits for the farm. For example, with more integrated systems of crops, livestock and forestry, Cuban farms are able to produce food while relying on minimal external inputs such as fuel and fertilizer. In addition, on-farm production of solar power and biogas from livestock manure has resulted in more reliable energy sources, buffering some farmers against energy crises…

Agricultural conservation practices deliver important benefits for the broader landscape. For example, agriculture in Cuba… constitutes a sizeable share of the overall landscape, [and they] are realizing the importance of watershed-wide planning. Another broader landscape benefit is to wildlife. For example, Cuba's forestry sector is increasing its focus on planting native trees to benefit local wildlife. Thoughtfully managed, farms and forests can connect, rather than fragment, natural areas that are critical for supporting climate-resilient biodiversity.

Experiences from Cuba… reveal how policy and finance can support sustainable agriculture. For example, Cuba is researching payment for ecosystem services approaches that could allow farmers engaging in sustainable agriculture to receive compensation for the landscape-scale benefits they provide. Assigning economic value to outcomes such as increased soil carbon or improved wildlife habitat would incentivize both conservation practices and data collection more generally, which is essential for science-based policymaking.

FF:
We need to generate agricultural systems that are resilient to whatever climatic event. And if the agricultural system is biodiverse, if it is heterogeneous, and having the capacity to mitigate the effects of any of these events, then it can be more sustainable. More sustainable from the economic, ecological and social point of view.

But it is an uphill struggle, trying to change not just the policies of those in power – and ensuring that resources are invested in the most sustainably effective way – but also in changing the consciousness of the population as a whole.

AM:
There are programmes for taking care of the environment. Certainly in terms of education, because a lot of information is given – on the television and in the press. But the population doesn't assimilate it.

There is such a lack of values, of consciousness in the population right now; and in our municipality there is a marked dehumanisation. Indiscipline. Indifference. It is a lamentable situation. Critical. But yes, those programmes do exist, and they try to have an effect. But there are obstacles, sometimes because of the local leadership not giving this the attention they should. Alluding to the lack of resources, the lack of one thing or the other.

AF:
Undoubtedly there is a problem of a lack of resources, because of the US economic blockade of the island. Also because of all the cultural problems that the country has. There have been a lot of political attempts trying to change the import culture of Cuba. For a long time we were dependent upon Comecon and the Soviet Union, and whatever was needed was imported. Then, in the 1990s, there was the crisis, and this declined somewhat. But afterwards the idea remerged that it was better to buy outside the country than to produce here. This is an economic vision that has to change. And I think that this is a moment for change, because undoubtedly there are enormous economic restrictions. Because of the impediments to accessing sources of finance, for example. Sometimes financing is approved for something, and afterwards the finance is cut, because there is an element that isn't allowed.

To give you an example, it has now been a few years that there has been a platform here prospecting for oil, brought from I don't know where. And this platform was stuck for three months in Trinidad and Tobago, while the North Americans carried out inspections to see whether it had a screw that came from the US. And well, when they proved that it didn't, that everything was, I think, English, or European, then the platform arrived, did its job, and then left. Which is to say that the United States, with respect to Cuban economic problems, impedes the development of stable and permanent policies. It forces us to be looking here and there for what is needed.

That's not the only problem. There are also internal problems. And there are problems that sometimes are inexplicable, in terms of the implementation of decisions that have nothing to do with the outside world. They are ours, and nevertheless we can't see them. That's why I stress that there are problems of political cultural vision, and of culture.

AM:
Yes, there are plans. Yes, projects do exist. And yes, programmes exist. But it is sometimes very difficult to carry these out. Because of objective and subjective questions – and it's the subjective that are the most damaging.

Although there is much to be done, there is a growing awareness in Cuba – at all levels – of the need not only to have appropriate policies in place, but for these to be matched to the specific situation of each locality.

AF:
In the first years of the twenty-first century, a very important project was carried out, which was the study of the risks and vulnerabilities of every municipality in the country. That is, every municipality had a risk and vulnerability protocol for its territory. And this was logically seen as a basis for subsequently developing local policies in relation to the large-scale environmental events that were affecting Cuba. Amongst those, hurricanes.

We also have to take into account that Cuba is affected by processes of desertification and drought, and the climatic variability of rain. That is, sometimes it rains a lot and at other times it hardly rains at all. The rain isn't distributed. In dry periods and in spring, it isn't distributed as it normally was forty years ago. And logically all this has an impact on local environments. As a result, a lot of work is being done with local governments to establish specific policies in every territory in order to deal with the local changes imposed by climate change.

Deriving from this microstudy that was carried out nationally concerning vulnerability and risk, it was determined, for example, that several cities and towns that are on the Cuban coasts (and whoever knows Cuba, realises that the largest part of the Cuban population is a coastal population), amongst them Caibarién, are very affected by climate change due to the elevation of the sea level, by meteorological events like hurricanes, and logically by the environmental variations caused by this whole situation in the long term. Now work is trying to be done in conjunction with these populations. Trying to encourage them to move to higher ground, further inland, so that they aren't so affected by the proximity of the sea.

As you will realise, this is a major challenge, because a place like Caibarién is a town with a very long cultural tradition of fishing. It would involve changing the whole sociocultural perception of that town and its economic activities towards agriculture. And this is something that is very difficult.

Something similar occurs in, for example, Santa Cruz del Sur, in Camagüey, which has also been repeatedly affected by hurricanes – costing more than three thousand deaths in the hurricane of 1933, which has remained imprinted in the memory of the population and the local culture. Despite that, the population is resistant to moving. In Santa Cruz, they proposed moving the town 17 km inland, and the inhabitants said that they didn't want to go that far. Because if they just went 7 km, the sea wouldn't reach them. And they tried not to lose their marine connection.

There is really a contradiction that I don't see a solution for, not in the short term, and not in the coming years. Undoubtedly the natural changes on the global level now have a public character. That is, any kind of environmental change is going to impact on the population, and take on a public character. If it is not taken like this, if instead it is taken with a technocratic vision, it is going to be hard to find a solution.

New buildings, away from coast, Caibarién (2019)
Photo: Wilder Llanes Méndez

AF:
I believe that perhaps not all, but some populations perhaps won't necessarily have to leave the coast, but it will be necessary to carry out works in order to preserve that type of community, and avoid a greater impact from environmental changes.

Attention is also being given to the kinds of structures that are being built – so that these may be more resilient to the anticipated climatic events and rising sea levels.

AF:
I think that alternatives need to be looked for in different directions. One of these is in traditional structures, such as those that here were built on top of poles, and perhaps that would provide some means of mitigating, of adapting to environmental changes.

LN:
We have made a number of videos that deal with the theme, for example, of rescuing tradition. Fortunately in Cuba there is much knowledge about the original communities, most of which were exterminated but nevertheless there is much that remains in the geographical toponomy of Cuba. Many of their construction techniques have been maintained: the hut (*bohío*); and the use of the *vara en tierra* [rod in ground], which is a construction that is typical of Cuba and which was used in the yards of houses to preserve what was of most value to a family – their smaller livestock, some important goods. It has been proved that these buildings are practically impossible to damage.

AF:
As an example, perhaps not applicable to the whole nation, but at least here, in this coastal zone of Vedado. This is the zone that gets flooded. They are building an enormous hotel, here on the Malecón, precisely at the place that most frequently gets flooded. How to avoid that? Well, I think that there is a hundred-million-dollar project, something like that, to make a kind of barrier on the seafront. I am not sure if it will be in the water or on the embankment, but it is intended to prevent the zone from being flooded when hurricanes and high tides come.

Design for hurricane-proof traditional 'vara en tierra'
Image taken promotional video, Fundación Antonio Núñez Jiménez

MI:
They say that technology will always find a solution for problems. It's true that sometimes a scientific discovery is made, the engineer converts it into an application, and energy is saved, for example, where this was not even dreamed of before. The invention of cells for solar power, for example.

AF:
Now what happens is that there is a connection between research and local politics. For this reason [Cuban president] Diaz Canel is putting so much emphasis on supporting the universities, and the local research centres.

If the environment is to be used in a sustainable way, such that future generations may continue to benefit from it, new methods of exploiting resources in a less aggressive way are needed. Take, for example, fishing:

MI:
In Cuba, fishing habits have been changed, to eliminate the system of trawling, which was really destructive – and didn't recognise what was down below. It might as easily be a piece of coral, as a lobster, or a fish. It was a negative system for the sea, for the life in the sea, the marine life. Here it is banned.

MI:
But of course, the prohibition can't simply say, you can't do that anymore, go and die of hunger. What are the people who live from this supposed to do? So I know that there have been several solutions, amongst them giving to these fishing communities boats equipped with other technology so that they can maintain a good recovery. Give special equipment to these people.

In the case of Carahatas, which is a zone in the north of central Cuba, where sponges are common. They are abundant. It's possible to create a sponge farm. They make a line, with trenches, and sow sponges there. They leave them, and they grow. And afterwards they can be collected, and sown again, and that is a reproduction in natural conditions, although assisted.

While the ideas, and in some quarters the political will, is certainly present, much needs to be done to ensure that this effectively transposes into action.

AF:
But how do local governments deal with this situation? By intervening. Why do they do that? Because of the centralist vision of the local government. We have had sixty years of centralised, authoritarian politics, and that is the culture. You can find a local government that acts as if it were a ministry. Sometimes the ministry itself is easier to talk with and give answers than the local government.

I don't want to say that all are the same, but there are those that are like that. So in this sense, changing the political vision of the local government is fundamental. Until the government – not just in the sense of climate change but in every sense of the application of policies by local government – until the local government stops seeing themselves as public functionaries, and that they owe their position to the population and not to the higher levels, then Cuban politics is not going to change. That is, there is a need to turn things on their head.

RF:
I think there is a political will on the part of the government to prioritise these themes. There is a will on the part of the institutions that are dedicated to these themes in Cuba. And there are many people who really consider that it is fundamental to protect what surrounds us. The environment that surrounds us, that offers us such important resources, such as through ecotourism, and other kinds of activities as well. I believe also that the government has given a lot of attention to the creation of a large network of scientific institutions, that has turned its attention to the environmental challenge facing the country as a result of climate change. For example, tourism of sun and beach is one of the most threatened by the rising sea levels, the erosion of the beaches, and I think that the government is very conscious of the need to preserve these resources.

AF:
I think that Diaz Canel at least has things clear. When he was First Party Secretary in Villa Clara, he was somebody who listened a lot. I had the experience of carrying out research in El Condado, which is a marginal neighbourhood in Santa Clara. At three in the morning I was in the house of the family doctor in El Condado, and we heard a very big commotion. People talking loudly. What was happening?

Caibarién seen from the air (2018)
Aerial photograph by Ariel Suárez, courtesy of Giselle García Castro

AF:
When I went out, there were Diaz Canel and Humberto (who was the President of the provincial government) sitting on the sidewalk talking with people. The people came out of their houses to tell them the problems that they had in the neighbourhood. So this is somebody who listens, and who knows how to manage local themes.

But he can't resolve them on his own. There has to be a team that will need to be slowly put together, because probably in Cuban politics, like in all political systems, there are internal contradictions. One person thinks one way, another thinks another, and all that has to be remodelled.

MN:
In 2017, the Cuban state approved what is known as *Tarea Vida* [Project Life] which is a state project to be carried out over the short, medium and long term. Short term until 2030. Medium term until 2050. Long term until 2100. In this there is a whole collection of activities in which a whole series of organisations and institutions are involved, with a financial contribution to try to minimise the impact of climate change.

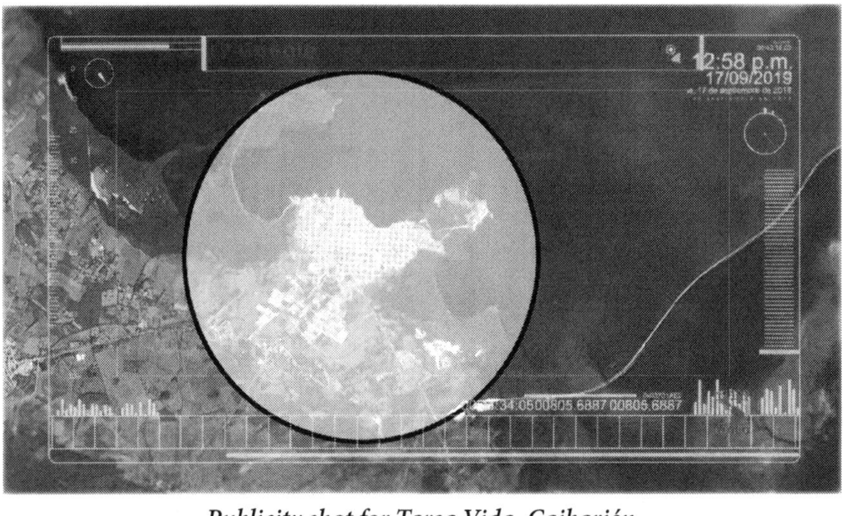

Publicity shot for Tarea Vida, Caibarién
Image taken from film *Cuba: Living Between Hurricanes*

LN:
Fortunately, there then came a state plan for confronting climate change: the *Tarea Vida*. This has been articulated as a state plan in every circumstance, and to all sectors and all organisations of the central administration of the state, saying how each one – according to their activity within society, the economy or production – were going to incorporate the variables of climate change and the incidence of extreme climatological events. I think that this has been very revolutionary in the articulation of the state in all its elements, and the incorporation of the environmental theme within its plans.

AF:
Tarea Vida is a series of public policies being carried out in a number of directions for local improvement, and adaptation to climate change. In every territory, according to the peculiarities of every territory.

Amongst its strategic actions, the *Tarea Vida* has established the following measures: banning new constructions on endangered coasts, and reducing the demographic density in low-lying coastal areas; developing construction methods appropriate for flood-prone areas; adapting farming activities, changing land use and reducing the area under cultivation in affected zones; crop diversification and improving soil conditions; and reorganising coastal settlements, including the recuperation of beaches and reforestation. Caibarién is one of the areas falling under the plan.

MN:
A study was made of the most vulnerable regions, and those most likely to be affected by this climate change. And our coastal zone of Caibarién, and all the keys, are within these prioritised zones. A number of actions have already been carried out. Those of highest priority. Sand has been added to the beaches on the keys. The mangrove belt has been reforested as a protective curtain against the penetration of the sea and the salinisation of the water table.

And all this has happened in an economic context, with a need for resources to continue developing all these activities, in which environmental education plays an essential part.

AM:
In the lowest lying parts of Caibarién, those that are going to disappear in a question of decades, they are prohibiting the construction of buildings – whether privately or by the state. In fact, if you walk around Caibarién you will see that all the building work, all the urban conglomerations, are being distanced to the South, to the higher grounds.

But work, for example, on dykes, on engineering projects to hold back the sea, or at least ameliorate the damage: I don't see that they are doing any of that yet.

AAG:
Mangroves have already begun to grow beside the causeway. This is good in the sense that mangroves are ecological niches, habitats that are very important for many species, and strengthen and protect the coasts, even forming the coasts: the biogenic coasts made from mangroves or coral, or both.

AM:
The mangroves, and all the coastal vegetation, were affected by Hurricane Irma, two years ago. But it is a temporary effect. The keys, for example, still maintain an ample mangrove vegetation. There is still no cause for alarm. Also, replanting of mangroves is being carried out. I know this, because the mangroves not only are a natural refuge, and a very important link in the marine ecosystem, because of the large quantity of fauna that take refuge in them. But also because they are something with an economic use through the manufacture of charcoal; and the bark of red mangroves are used in the tanning industry, and in the pharmaceutical industry. So although they have been affected, I at least haven't seen cause for alarm.

If the measures that are being put into place are to succeed, then there will be a need for the community as a whole to play their part. Often many of the most visible examples of environmental decay are simply caused by a lack of consciousness of the problems on the part of the population as a whole. For this, social education is needed.

Mangroves, Caibarién (2019)
Photo: Gonzalo Vidal

LN:
Another of the questions that we draw attention to, is to try, with training workshops through the communication media, to eliminate the perception that nature is what causes damage. That nature is dangerous, when in reality nature is fulfilling its role. Because if it wasn't for nature, then we wouldn't be here. If there are hurricanes, if there are earthquakes, then it is part of a living organism – which is what the Earth is. And humans have to understand that it is they who have interrupted those processes through the urban development of production; and one has to live looking for solutions based on nature, and not confronting nature. These are conceptions that come from centuries ago, and I think that they need to be stressed, because they are still not well incorporated within the business world, nor any system whether socialist or capitalist. Although capitalism makes this more pressing due to the strength of consumerism. But I believe that it is a challenge for every social system.

MN:
There is an educational programme, that implicitly includes an element of environmental education. But I think that this still needs to be strengthened, along with the broadcasting over the mass media, print press, radio, television – because we need this in order to be able to survive these changes in the climate.

The *Fundación Antonio Nuñez Jiménez*, has been at the forefront of putting into practice the good environmental intentions, and working towards a more sustainable future for Cuba, its local communities and ecosystem. The Foundation is an NGO, dedicated to continuing the legacy of Antonio Nuñez Jiménez – a revolutionary leader, who carried out extensive first-hand research of Cuba's natural environment.

Fundación Antonio Núñez Jiménez, Havana, Cuba (2019)
Photo: Hannah Shami (courtesy of The Cuba Project, TigerLily Media & Jacksonville University)

LN:
We don't choose one sector or another to work with. The most important part of the mission of the *Fundación* is to work towards a culture of nature, with the difficult and complex objective of harmonising society and its environment. When we say society, we include every sector of it. Every level, whether communal, municipal or provincial government, science academies or scientific sector, business sector. The new entrepreneurs that in Cuba are the new economic actors that are emerging. And we don't exclude any, because nature does not exclude anyone. Nature touches us all evenly. So we can't exclude nor prioritise one group over another.

For us, the coasts are a priority, but then we have many priorities. For example, the work in cities and the vulnerability of cities is also a priority for us. Not only the coasts, but the marine zones. And the forests are also a priority, and seeds, and the themes of consumption, and the preservation of archives as well. We are being faithful to that holistic spirit of Núñez, trying to have a balance without hierarchy.

MI:
I am very keen that at some point we may succeed in bringing fully into normal education, from primary on, teaching about preparation for natural events that might be potentially disastrous. This ought to be a knowledge just like mathematics, physics, chemistry and biology. As far as I'm concerned, when a young person graduates from primary or secondary, they ought to have knowledge about the planet on which they live, about the Earth on which they live, and what the non-social dangers are that they have to confront daily.

Why? Well, because that person might one day be a businessperson, making decisions that don't just concern them, a father or mother with a family. That person may come to have a political position, and then represents a part of the world, of society. They become a part of international institutions.

And I think, or perhaps dream, that perhaps if I succeed in giving that person a culture that is sensitive to nature, which is precisely what Núñez Jiménez wanted, and a culture of preservation, and that person knows the value of a tree, an insect. Has knowledge about that. Well I imagine that he would be more positive in his actions, and would make better decisions for the preservation of humanity, but also for the preservation of nature.

AM:
I think that what is fundamental, what ought to exist, what ought to be plentiful, which should overflow the glasses in which it is held, is conscience. It is interest. It is the willingness for everyone to work – just as much the person who throws the rubbish into the street, as the government, whether municipal, provincial or national. That they find motivation, so that it can really be a conscientious and practical interest. For it not to remain on paper, in digital programmes, nor anything like that, but that it is put into practice. For it to leave the meeting tables, the meeting rooms, and be taken out into nature, to the earth, to the sea. Here. So that it can be made practical. Because many things can be done. There is need. There is a lack of resources. But I believe that the resource that is most needed is consciousness and a desire to really do things, and to do them well.

After all, it is not the environment, or the planet, or its climate, that is the real problem. Rather it is how we choose to interact with it. Whether we are capable of living in harmony with what surrounds us.

MI:
There is an historic contradiction between human society and nature. Society arrives in a place, occupies a space, and while it solves a problem for itself, as society, it creates a problem for the environment where it is. It upsets the environment. If you start to fish a lot, one day there will be an end to fishes. Because you were fishing incorrectly. You went beyond the capacity of the resources that you were exploiting.

And this applies everywhere. Nature is there. There was a time in which there was the false concept that it was there for us to make use of. That it is a commodity that I can use whenever I want. I pull down that mountain, and we fabricate all the cement that the world needs, to make another mountain of cement, of concrete. We dig deeply to bring out all the resources of the Earth. We are always transforming the Earth. And the Earth is prepared for this. The Earth is always transforming itself. But if we modify the environment in which we live too much, then the point will be reached in which the environment becomes hostile for us. And it is our fault.

In other places, in the mountains, we arrive, we cut down the trees. We fill them with buildings, with roads, with crops, etcetera. Monoculture. Monoculture in turn generates, when there is a lot of monoculture, more plagues. Imagine it, when a mosquito gets amongst two hundred people, it says this is paradise for the mosquito. It walks here, it walks there. Here it has its food guaranteed. So we generate the plague ourselves, with the large-scale monocultures, the large farms where there are two thousand chickens. My god, the virus that is interested in the chicken is very happy there. That is to say, we create the problems. And afterwards, well, we have the consequences. That's why the only solution that I can see for humanity is that we have to have the intelligence to act towards the preservation of the environment, and the care of ourselves. And these two things are not distinct. That is what humanity needs. Science needs to create knowledge, so that knowledge may allow intelligent decisions to be made from the political and social point of view. And then education has to be taken not only to adults, but to every level, so that a behavioural culture can be developed.

Every year on 5th June, World Environment Day is celebrated. On this day in 2020, the Director General of the Environment Agency of the Cuban Ministry of Science, Technology and Environment (CITMA) expressed a principle that will need to be present in the design of future Cuban policies: "the interconnection of the natural world with society." Or as Armando Fernández expressed it: "The relationship of science and politics must recognise that Cuban territory is limited and all relationships we establish on it have a finite character and a 'load capacity' that cannot be exceeded."

AM:
If the plans are carried out. If the consciousness of man is awakened and interest is awakened, then yes, we are going to improve things. Because the programmes that exist are good. And necessity has to make us take action. The blows that are being suffered due to the scourge of the hurricanes that are every time more frequent and with greater intensity, have got to teach us. They have to awaken the consciousness and the lack of interest that exists in many people, so as to be able to make these plans reality. That's in the first instance.

AM:
And in the second, well, education needs to really reach people: the educational message. It needs to reach those people who can contribute their grain of sand. Not to leave that plastic bag on the beach, on the coast, in a ditch. That is what needs to be avoided, as a question of consciousness.

Pioneering enterprises like Finca Marta are leading the way, and demonstrating just how old wisdoms and new technologies and science can be brought together with political will, an entrepreneurial spirit, and social and environmental conscience, to bring hope for the future.

FF:
The well is a symbol for our project, because on the one hand it demonstrates and confirms our desire to put in the effort needed not only to transform the farm, but to transform the territory. The transformation of the territory comes as a consequence of the demonstration of what we have achieved here. And this well was the start. We spent seven months breaking rocks manually to make it, and after seven months we found the water. Almost fifteen metres deep. We found water here in these rocky hills, where nobody thought we would find water. And we had sufficient water to develop our economic life here. From here, our animals have drunk water, our bees, we have used water for irrigation, and it has also served as drinking water, because the water has a very good quality.

But the well has another kind of relevance. It is a metaphor, in which are joined the old and the new. This is a rustic well, precarious. It cost us a lot of physical effort. A labour that few people would be prepared to do these days. Nevertheless, finishing the well we had the possibility of installing a solar-powered pump. And within the well we have very modern technology to pump the water, making use of the renewable energy.

Another of the limitations that we had was the rocks. We had a lot of rocks in the ground, and so we made piles of rocks throughout the farm, and used them to make different buildings. We made the cattle shed, we made the foundations of the house with the stones, we also made the whole of the terrace with rocks. That is to say, something that seemed to be a problem, was turned into a resource.

***Well, Finca Marta* (2019)**

Image taken from documentary *Cuba: Living Between Hurricanes*

The animals come here in the evening, and they spend the whole of the night here. They spend about twelve hours inside the cattle shed, and the following day we clean the cattle shed, and collect the manure. The manure with water is the primary material for the production of biogas, and the production of bio-fertilisers. So here in the cattle shed, the energy and nutrition cycles are closed.

Then there is the *piñon florido* (*Gliricidio sepium*) – a tree that provides very high quality fodder, having more than 20 percent protein, and the animals find it very palatable. The animals like it a lot. In spring, we cut the branches, and we give them to the animals. So that the trees don't grow too high, but also taking advantage of the biomass. We have about ten thousand trees around the farm. Imagine how much biomass that is. It's a traditional practice. But also we are researching into it, and it is one of the important alternatives for the tropics. In the tropics, trees play a fundamental role, because not only do they provide the fodder, but they also give shade for the cattle. And it also produces a lot of flowers. We have bees, and when this flowers in February and March, it results in a dense, dark honey, with a very high quality. When we talk of the trees, when we talk about the different components of the system, we are talking about the concept of multifunctionality. Every component of the system plays several different parts.

Fernando Funes, owner of Finca Marta, with piñon florido (2019)
Image taken from documentary *Cuba: Living Between Hurricanes*

AM:
There are plans, and I have faith. I have hope, and hope is green. It's green because it stands for nature. For the love that I have for nature.

FF:
I believe that we have a blockade at a world level, and the world is now living through a Special Period. There are many reasons why we need change in the world's agricultural system, and it is necessary – not only in Cuba, but in every country of the world – to rethink agriculture along other lines. To rethink not only how food is produced, but how agriculture connects to the rest of society. And there are many people working on this. Many people around the world, from their own communities, with their own difficulties and their own problems, not only related to technology and how food is produced, but also economic and social changes. And also the impact climate change has had. The impact that there has been from the imbalances and variability in the climate – not just in Cuba, but anywhere in the world. Access to water. Prolonged droughts. The passing of hurricanes or tornados, and different climatic events that affect agriculture, are no more than a response by nature to the bad management of these natural resources.

If we succeed in establishing agricultural systems that are more respectful of the environment, but which are also more socially viable, equal and fair, then we can think of the world having a sustainable future.

There are things that are imposed by life itself, because of the circumstances, that mean that often there is no other alternative. And that is the situation today. There is no other alternative for those that don't listen than to accept that this model that we are proposing from many perspectives in the world, of an agriculture related to the environment, and environmental protection, and respecting all forms of life – that this is the path that will make possible the continued survival of the human species on the Earth.

Caibarién: "The world can be saved if we each play our part" (2019)
Photo: Gonzalo Vidal

Afterword

Jean Stubbs

"Some compare what's coming with a Category 5 hurricane."

Since launching *Cuba: Living Between Hurricanes* among colleagues during the Havana Film Festival in December 2019, one of the many challenges the Covid-19 pandemic threw our way was having to adapt to online screenings of the documentary followed by Q&A and keeping abreast of the many developments in Cuba, which none when filming could possibly have seen coming.

We set out to make a thought-provoking documentary, and discussions after each screening point to us certainly having done so. They have been related to the documentary itself, but also the impact of the pandemic – not least having brought Cuba's economic lifeline of international tourism to an abrupt halt. Health was not an issue touched on in the documentary, though we knew of Cuba's track record in public health, nationally and internationally. Cuba rose swiftly and effectively to the challenge at home and abroad, sending Cuban medics to aid countries across the globe. International tourism, which did feature centrally in the documentary, was altogether another story. The Cuban government, like other governments around the world, closed the borders to international travel and, thus, tourism. This, coupled with the toll of the US Trump administration further tightening the noose of the 60-year US embargo, hit Cuba hard. Remittances from Cubans abroad, mainly in the United States, were severely curtailed; US-friendly governments such as those in Brazil and Ecuador were swayed to end their Cuban medic programmes, though some were later reinstated; and heavy US pressure was put on Venezuela to stop oil shipments to Cuba.

Much of our filming had centered around Caibarién in north-central Villa Clara province, and in May 2020 the central town of Sanctí Spíritus, in the neighbouring province of the same name, was a regional Covid hotspot. *Escambray*, the local town newspaper, carried an interview by two of its reporters with the President of the National Association of Economists, Oscar Luis Hung Pentón, about the economic fallout and options facing Cuba as a result of the pandemic. A question inevitably raised was the outlook for Cuba's international tourism. As we explored in the documentary, Cuba has a long history of commodity exports, with the rise and fall of commodity frontiers linked to social and environmental degradation and a vulnerability to global markets. International tourism had, in effect, become Cuba's most recent commodity frontier. Like preceding frontiers, it was not without social and environmental costs and was highly susceptible to world market conditions beyond Cuba's control. Covid showed that with a vengeance.

Hung Pentón's reply back in May 2020 is worth citing here:

> Now is the opportunity for an alliance between tourism and health. Cuba needs to develop health tourism more strategically, with linkages to agriculture and industry. I believe tourism can retool to become a model based on nature and health. This is no time for grand hotels with communal pools, restaurants with buffet service, or tourism crowding our towns and cities.

His words were prescient. Two months later, in July 2020, as the Cuban government moved to a phased lifting of Covid lockdown, a two-track strategy was announced of allowing domestic tourism on the mainland while restricting international tourism to the natural environment of the offshore keys, with stringent health requirements and monitoring. The strategy came alongside a raft of economic reforms, many of them agreed a decade earlier though not implemented. These included greater autonomy for an expanding domestic private sector, a reinvigorated programme for supporting industrial production and more leasing of land to bolster smallholder agriculture, with stronger linkages between the various sectors, all to be undertaken in an environmentally friendly way.

Havana then saw a worrying resurgence of Covid, which took the city back into lockdown. In early August, an interesting news items that made the front-page of the national daily *Granma* was the action plan for Caibarién that had been given government approval earlier in the year. Addressing several of the issues raised in the documentary, it ended on a cautionary note: how this moves forward would "depend on how the plan is taken up by the authorities, how people are involved, and of course the objective conditions of the country." Conditions proved far from conducive.

By late 2020, faced with an increasingly difficult economic situation, the Cuban government risked opening up completely to international travel and allowing home stays as well. This resulted in an increase in Covid-19 cases, hospitalisations and deaths on a scale not seen during 2020, especially in Havana but also across the island, and the race was on for Cuba to trial and roll out its own Covid vaccines. The November 2020 US election ushering in the Biden administration brought a glimmer of hope on the international horizon, though none foresee an early end to the US embargo.

Further economic reforms in early 2021 included the long-anticipated monetary reform, which left the Cuban peso in effect a devalued domestic currency. Prices of basic foodstuffs and other necessities (when available) doubled, tripled and quadrupled, beyond the means of many. Measures have been taken to mitigate this with salary increases in the state sector, but those in what before the pandemic had been a growing private sector lost out, and many others fell outside any net.

Worryingly for environmentalists, the effort to boost domestic food supplies extended to government approval for controlled GM farming, when initial experiments had been opposed by agronomists and organic farmers over a decade earlier. Also, mass tourism continued to be the panacea in the eyes of some, including a megaproject in Pinar del Río, which many feared would have serious repercussions on the natural environment. The ultimate irony, perhaps, is that Cayo Santa María should have been listed number two in the world for its beaches and is the recipient of small but increasing numbers of Russian tourists in the framework of a bilateral deal between

Cuba and Russia, while Caibarién lies off the radar of renewed national and international coastal resilience aid across the island.

Debate rages among economists, social scientists, environmentalists and people across Cuba as to why, when tourist capacity even before the pandemic already far exceeded demand, more isn't being diverted to invest in sustainable local agriculture. Views oscillate between optimism and despair. Will lessons be learnt from the perfect storm of the pandemic? Cuba, like the rest of the world, is at a crossroads. While current global strictures might sadly invoke a future that is less rather than more in harmony with nature, hopefully there are those around the world, as there are in Cuba (and as evidenced in the documentary and this book), who can make a difference in the struggle to make the latter a reality.

Acknowledgments

I would like to thank all those involved in the making of the film, *Cuba: Living Between Hurricanes* – without which this book would never have been made. First and foremost, Michael Chanan, for his directing and editing, and putting up with production conditions that were far from optimal, and minimally funded; and my co-writer and co-producer, Jean Stubbs. The two of them have since been at the forefront of screening the documentary, and participating in the numerous Q&A sessions (on-line, and once the restrictions caused by the global pandemic have been lifted, in person).

Thanks to the Arts and Humanities Research Council (AHRC), without whose funding the film (and thereby this book) would never have been made. Also our Cuban partners, the *Fundación Antonio Núñez Jiménez* (FANJ) (and President Liliana Núñez Jiménez) and the *Instituto Cubano del Arte e Industria Cinematográficos* (ICAIC) (in particular Dolores Calviño, for the pre-selection of the footage), for the practical support that they provided us with; likewise the Institute of Latin American Studies (ILAS, now the Centre for Latin American and Caribbean Studies, CLACS), at the University of London, for the administrative and institutional support given (and the logistical assistance there of Penelope Elvy, Valerie James and Bertha Archer).

In Cuba, our advisers on the ground, Reinaldo Funes Monzote (representing FANJ, and who took us to the ecotourist installation at Las Terrazas, and not far away Finca Marta – a model of sustainable farming run by his brother Fernando), and Pedro Manuel González Reinoso (our man in Caibarién); also Gonzalo Vidal, for his photography, and for his practical experience helping us with arrangements – a continuation for him and me of many years of creative collaboration and friendship. A big thank you too for the participation of all others who were prepared to be interviewed, and whose words are what both the documentary and this book have been constructed from: Armando Caymares, Armando Fernández Soriano, Abel Arnaldo González López, Angel Luis Díaz Cabezas, Alejandro Morffi González, Angel Omar Vara San Juan, Ana Vera Estrada, Fernando Funes Monzote, Hernán Venegas Delgado, Luis Enrique Ramos Guadalupe, Manuel Iturralde-Vinent, Martín Núnez Rodríguez, Mireya Pérez, Natalia Quintana Díaz, Oscar Zanetti Lecuona, Raúl Rodríguez Cabrera, Sherry Johnson, Juan Emerio Sánchez Freire and Nancy E. Martínez Abreu.

The film itself could not have been made without the creative input (and excellent, always upbeat company) of Ilmi Pérez Stubbs, for his superb camera work and graphics; and post-production editing by Luciano Piazza. Thanks also to the *Cinemateca de Cuba*, for providing access to their extensive archives; and Giselle García Castro for making available to us drone footage from her own documentary, *Lista Quinta*. Also for their various inputs along the way: Pedro Pérez Sarduy, Ash Johann, Mercedes Pérez Armenteros, Aldo Misael Morffi Noa, Elieser Turó González, María Elena Villegas Martín and Raisa Guevarra García; Gustavo Muñoz Alvarez and Amado Gutierrez Brunet, for getting us places in Havana and Caibarién; and the Hostal Sunrise for their hospitality during our time filming there.

Finally, all those who participated in the workshop held at the outset of filming at FANJ in Havana; at the subsequent work-in-progress screenings there and in Remedios; and the various screenings and Q&A sessions that have happened around the world since.

Further Reading

Sergio Diaz-Briquets, *Conquering Nature: The Environmental Legacy of Socialism in Cuba* (University of Pittsburgh Press, 2000)

Michael Chanan, *Cuban Cinema* (University of Minnesota Press, 2004)

Jonathan Curry-Machado, *Cuban Sugar Industry: Transnational Networks and Engineering Migrants in Mid-Nineteenth Century Cuba* (Palgrave Macmillan, 2011)

Kerry Emanuel, *Divine Wind: The History and Science of Hurricanes* (Oxford University Press, 2005)

Reinaldo Funes Monzote, *From Rainforest to Cane Field: An Environmental History since 1492* (University of North Carolina Press, 2008)

Sherry Johnson, *Climate and Catastrophe in Cuba and the Atlantic World in the Age of Re volution* (University of North Carolina Press, 2011)

Louis A. Pérez, *Winds of Change: Hurricanes and the Transformation of Nineteenth-Century Cuba* (University of North Carolina Press, 2001)

Luis Enrique Ramos Guadalupe, *Father Benito Viñes: The 19th-Century Life and Contributions of a Cuban Hurricane Observer and Scientist* (American Meteorological Society, 2014)

Peter Rosset & Medea Benjamin, *The Greening of the Revolution: Cuba's Experiment with Organic Agriculture* (Ocean Press, 1994)

Stuart B. Schwartz, *Sea of Storms: A History of Hurricanes in the Greater Caribbean from Columbus to Katrina* (Princeton University Press, 2015)

Pamela Stricker, *Toward a Culture of Nature: Environmental Policy and Sustainable Development in Cuba* (Lexington Books, 2007)
Jean Stubbs, *Tobacco on the Periphery: A Case Study in Cuban Labour History, 1860-1958* (Cambridge University Press, 1985)
David Taylor, Scott Slovic & Armando Fernández Soriano (eds), *An Island in the Stream: Ecocritical and Literary Responses to Cuban Environmental Culture* (Lexington Books, 2019)
Julia E. Wright, *Sustainable Agriculture and Food Security in an Era of Oil Scarcity.* Lessons from Cuba (Earthscan, 2009)
Oscar Zanetti, *Sugar and Railroads* (University of North Carolina Press, 1998)

Index

Entries in **bold** refer to illustrations. The interviewees have been listed, with references to their interview statements in *italics*, subdivided by chapter.

I

J

K

L

M

N

O

P

Also published by Amaurea Press

Anna Lidia Vega Serova, *Un jardin en miniatura/A Miniature Garden.*

Poetry from Cuba, with colour photographs by Gonzalo Vidal. Spanish, with English translation by Jonathan Curry-Machado (ISBN 978-1-914278-00-6).

"While I look at these images, I imagine that they play with time, they romp with the present disolving into the mists of the past; while the poetry sings of what could be in the elusive and chimeric future."
(Racso Morejón)

"Anna Lidia tells her stories from the perspective of someone who knows that she will not be able to change the imperfect, rotten and contaminating reality. She simply tells of what is dirty, smelly, low, treacherous in that reality, starting from the damaging, malign, mephistophelic connotations of modernity in the individual who is marked by fate."
(Amir Valle)

www.amaurea.co.uk

Printed in Great Britain
by Amazon

62769218R00161